AUNTIE MAME

A New Play
BY JEROME LAWRENCE AND ROBERT E. LEE

Based on the best-selling
novel by Patrick Dennis

★

★

DRAMATISTS
PLAY SERVICE
INC.

SPECIAL NOTE

AUTHORS' PRODUCTION NOTES

The scenic plan has been considerably simplified for this version of AUNTIE MAME. There should be one standing set, the living-room of the Beekman Place Apartment. Several of the flats should have panels in them, which can be changed during the course of the play, as Mame's taste in decor changes. Pieces of furniture also should be changed through the course of the play.

Both bedrooms (Mame's and the Peckerwood bedroom) plus a paperhanging scene have been eliminated in this version, thus saving some six scenic changes.

The doorway leading to the foyer of the apartment should be downstage L., a separate unit which can be moved on casters back and forth as the scenes demand it.

One black or neutral-colored drop or traveller is necessary, in front of which a variety of scenes can be played: Macy's, the telephone switch-board, the theatre scene, the four brief opening scenes of Act II, and the Upson patio scene.

One painted drop is necessary, covering all the Peckerwood scenes. But these can be played in a shallow one or two, downstage from your standing set.

The curving staircase on the Beekman Place set is of vital importance, and, if possible, the top should curve downstage, so that Mame's final climb with Michael is played toward the audience.

Where music is indicated, a lead sheet will be found at the end of the text. (The melodies of "Chu-Chin-Chow"; "St. Boniface Fight Song"; "O, Rumson U"; and "Tu Ra Loora Lay.")

* * * *

A great many parts are doubled in casting throughout the play. At the cocktail party, Osbert is a double for Mr. Loomis later on. Patrick, with a mustache and a turban, can be a party guest, along with Pegeen, Gloria, Sally Cato, Mr. Upson. In the New York production, our Agnes Gooch was also Radcliffe of the deep voice. The PAPER-HANGER, with an added mustache, becomes Dr. Shurr, the vet. Mrs. Upson doubles as one of the customers in Macy's. Her

3

son becomes Emory later on. Gloria, Mrs. Upson and others, in big hats, become part of the milling group at Peckerwood. Brian O'Bannion, facing upstage the entire time, becomes the LEADING MAN of the theatre-scene. Michael is, of course, Young Pat, with a red wig added. Bishop Eleftharosees, of the mitred beard, becomes the THEATRE MANAGER, with cigar, and Cousin Jeff, with Southern accent.

SCENIC BREAKDOWN

The standing set of BEEKMAN PLACE, with two of the walls panelled so they can be changed in the course of the play, has four doors in it. One is U.C. (to the kitchen), one is D.R., to the dining room; one is beneath the curving staircase, D.L., and the outside door, which is D.L. all the way to the proscenium opening. (This final door should be movable, so that it can be struck during the other scenes-in-one.) There is a mantlepiece upstage of the door R. The couch is usually angled in the D.R. area. The end table (used so often by Mame) is alongside the kitchen door.

ACT I

Scene 1: A movie-screen drop, in the event your curtain is not flat enough to take a slide projection. Your slide should look like a legal document. The voice (on public address system) should dramatize the provisions of the will, being exasperated as the copy indicates.

   The final slide of the CHICAGO TRIBUNE should approximate a newspaper as much as possible. In an emergency, only voices can be used, but it is not advised. In this event, the voice for the headline should be:
"News bulletin. Chicago, October 15th, 1928: Businessman Drops Dead in Steamroom of Chicago Athletic Club."

Scene 2: If you can afford a scrim curtain, it should be used here to mask the Beekman Place Apartment. Only the door downstage and the foyer area, decorated in Chinoiserie, should be seen. If you do not use a scrim, try your black curtain here and fly or draw it quickly at the end of this scene. The effect should be of Norah and Young Pat actually entering the apartment with the audience. If you use no curtain at all between the foyer and the apartment, try to confine your lighting to the foyer area alone, and quickly bring up the lights on the party as we move through the door. The door itself may be moved out of sight once they are through it.

Scene 3: The panels in this Beekman Place scene are of a Japanese nobleman committing hari-kari and one of Japanese birds and bridges, a typical oriental motif. The furniture should have a far-Eastern flavor.

Scene 4: The Hari-kari panel is the same. The other panel is now Cubistic, a wild array of modernistic blobs. The foyer door should be in place. The bar Young Pat works with should be D.L., and on wheels, so Young Pat can move it toward Babcock and take stage while he performs his martini-making bit. There should be an ice-bucket, a martini pitcher, and clearly apparent bottles of gin and vermouth on the bar.

Scene 5: The change should occur during darkness, with no curtain pulled, and only the ringing of the phone filling the slight pause. The final panel should be changed from the Hari-Kari picture to a modernistic portrait of a Madonna and Child.

Ito's "anatomical" chart should be a realistic medical chart.

The foyer door should be clearly visible. Improvise your own ridiculously Oriental-musical comedy style dance for Vera and Mame.

Scene 6: This can be played in front of your black curtain, with a row of spotlights angling up, approximating the theatre audience upstage. If possible, the backs of two flats can be used as masking at each side, or, lacking this, simple screens, which can be carried on and off. The bare work-light on the stage at the finish of the scene can be most effective.

Scene 7: This unit, a mock-up telephone switchboard, should be built with the board itself divided on two sides of the operator. The boards should angle outwards, toward the audience, so that Mame is, in effect, at the point of a letter V, the open end toward the audience. This unit should be on wheels so that it can be rolled on and off. The entire thing should be in front of your black curtain, with only a spotlight on it. The buzzes should be of two tones and keep coming throughout the scene. Play it stage left.

Scene 8: Again, a tiny unit on wheels—a single counter at MACY's, hung with roller-skates and Christmas lights. It plays in front of the black curtain. Perhaps a cut-out of the word "MACY'S" should be seen from the reverse angle. Thus, we the audience, see the back end of the counter. Mame makes her entrance clear across stage from left, with this unit oriented right, and again in only a spotted area.

6

Scene 9: Add only a Christmas tree to the Beekman Place set. As a sad version of "Deck the Halls" is playing, MAME crosses the full length of the stage, goes through the foyer door, and the apartment lights up as she enters. But turn the Christmas tree lights on first for an interesting effect.

Try to get your music and announcement piped right through the little radio on your set.

Scene 10: This can be a painted drop downstage of your black curtain. It should look as much like Tara of "Gone With the Wind" as possible: white columns, magnolias. Cut into the left side of the drop should be a curtained doorway, alongside of which is a Dutch window, the top open for the second Peckerwood scene.

Production note: if your Mother Burnside can't burp, put somebody who can behind the drop with a megaphone. With proper coordination, these "dubbed-in" burps work wonderfully.

Scene 11: The same, with just a spotlight on the area left.

Scene 12: The same, with lighting effect of dawn. Try, if possible, to get your sound-effects of the hunt out front. In the N.Y. production, speakers along the balcony rail gave a stereophonic effect. The final crash should be from a speaker off-stage L.

* * * *

ACT II

(The first four scenes are played before the black drop, in spotted areas, and should have the simplest outlines of scenic effects.)

Scene 1: A simple school desk. A spotlight on it. To give Young Pat some height, sit him on some books.

Scene 2: A spotted area stage left. A three-step inset, suggesting the Pyramids. This should be as simple as possible, with Beau beginning high on the top step, and Mame seated on the bottom.

Scene 3: The same as Scene 1, with possibly a different lamp. Again just a desk in the spotted area, right. Add a portable typewriter.

Scene 4: In front of the Scene 2 levels, place a cut-out of a steep mountain. Beau, again on the top level, is out of sight. Mame stands on the first step. The effect should be simple, but with an effect of height. Connect the ice-axe to a simple pulley at the upstage top edge of your mountain cut-out; swing the Alpinstock out, then let the rope dangle for a maximum comedy effect.

7

Scene 5: The Beekman Place standing set as before. Dustcovers over most of the furniture as the lights come up. A standard typewriter and a dictaphone have been added on a desk which is where the sofa used to be. A chaise longue is downstage left. The foyer-door should be visible.

Scene 6: The Beekman Place apartment, with the panels quickly changed to simulated huge bookcases filled with literary treasures. Add a bust of Shakespeare and perhaps Dickens.

Scene 7: Identical to Scene 6.

Scene 8: Identical to Scenes 6 and 7, with an indication that it is early morning.

Scene 9: In front of the black drop. The Upson Patio. If you have flying space and can afford an additional drop, you might want to use a painted drop of the Connecticut countryside, but it is not vital. There should be a portable bar, left, with some bar stools off stage ready for Upson to carry on. At center, on wheels, so that it can move easily in, is a country-type patio bench.

Scene 10: Beekman Place again, this time the panels changed to extreme modern. The couch, which Ito carries on, should be almost to the floor. There should be a wire hanging from above, to which the mobile can be attached. The foyer-door should be visible.

Scene 11: Beekman Place, as before, with a couple of packing boxes scattered around the room, prominently marked: "FROM MRS. M. LINDSAY WOOLSEY, PUNJAB, INDIA. TO MRS. M. LINDSAY WOOLSEY, 3 BEEKMAN PLACE, NEW YORK CITY." For the very end of the scene, the lights should all dim on the main stage and the only final source of light as Mame and Michael climb the stairs should be from the head of the stairs, as if they were climbing the Himalayas, heading into the morning sunrise.

JEROME LAWRENCE & ROBERT E. LEE.

AUNTIE MAME was first presented by Robert Fryer and Lawrence Carr on October 31, 1956, at the Broadhurst Theatre, New York City. The Production was designed by Oliver Smith. The play was directed by Morton DaCosta. The cast was as follows:

NORAH MULDOON ....*Beulah Garrick*
PATRICK DENNIS, as a boy ....*Jan Handzlik*
ITO ....*Yuki Shimoda*
VERA CHARLES ....*Polly Rowles*
OSBERT ....*Cris Alexander*
RALPH DEVINE ....*Grant Sullivan*
BISHOP ELEFTHAROSEES ....*William Martel*
M. LINDSAY WOOLSEY ....*John O'Hare*
AUNTIE MAME ....*Rosalind Russell*
MR. WALDO, a paper hanger ....*Geoffrey Bryant*
MR. BABCOCK ....*Robert Allen*
AL LINDEN, the stage manager ....*Wally Mohr*
A THEATRE MANAGER ....*William Martel*
ASSISTANT STAGE MANAGER ....*Duane Camp*
A MAID ....*Kip McArdle*
A BUTLER ....*Paul Lilly*
A LEADING MAN ....*James Field*
LORD DUDLEY ....*Walter Riemer*
A CUSTOMER ....*Kip McArdle*
A CUSTOMER'S SON ....*Barry Towsen*
MR. LOOMIS, a floor-walker ....*Chris Alexander*
BEAUREGARD JACKSON PICKETT BURNSIDE ....*Robert Smith*
COUSIN JEFF ....*William Martel*
COUSIN FAN ....*Nan McFarland*
COUSIN MOULTRIE ....*Frank Roberts*
SALLY CATO MACDOUGAL ....*Marian Winters*
EMORY MACDOUGAL ....*Barry Blake*
MOTHER BURNSIDE ....*Ethel Cody*
FRED, a groom ....*Paul Lilly*

9

SAM, another groom ....*James Field*
A HUNTSMAN ....*Cris Alexander*
DR. SHURR, a vet ....*Geoffrey Bryant*
PATRICK DENNIS, a young man ....*Robert Higgins*
AGNES GOOCH ....*Peggy Cass*
BRIAN O'BANNION ....*James Monks*
GLORIA UPSON ....*Joyce Lear*
DORIS UPSON ....*Dorothy Blackburn*
CLAUDE UPSON ....*Walter Klavun*
PEGEEN RYAN ....*Patricia Jenkins*
MICHAEL DENNIS ....*Jan Handzlik*

and a great many friends
of AUNTIE MAME

SYNOPSIS OF SCENES

The action of the play takes place in Auntie Mame's Beekman Place apartment and various other locales in which she becomes involved during a period of years from 1928 to 1946.

The Beekman Place Apartment

ACT I

SCENE 1

A projection appears on the curtain. It is a blow-up of a legal document: A voice on the P.A. speaks the words along with the projection:

"LAST WILL AND TESTAMENT

I, Edwin Dennis, being of sound mind and body, do hereby bequeath to my only son, Patrick, all my worldly possessions. In the event of my demise, I direct our faithful servant, Norah Muldoon, to deliver Patrick to my sister and next-of-kin, Mame Dennis, at 3 Beekman Place, New York City. The expenses of his upbringing shall be supervised by the Knickerbocker Bank as trustee, with the full power to keep that crazy sister of mine from doing anything too damned eccentric."

Behind this document, music begins to sound a trifle fey and Disney-esque.

"Since I keep myself in splendid physical condition through daily workouts at the Chicago Athletic Club, I am confident that these provisions will not go into force or effect for many years. I hereby affix my hand this fourteenth day of October, in the year 1928.

Signed:
EDWIN DENNIS"

There is a startled, eyebrow-lifting figure in the music, and the will slides out of sight, to be followed by a newspaper clipping, which reads:

"CHICAGO TRIBUNE—OCTOBER 15, 1928
BUSINESSMAN DROPS DEAD IN STEAMROOM
OF CHICAGO ATHLETIC CLUB"

(No voice on the headline.)

ACT I

Scene 2

Buzzing of a door bell, as the lights come up on the door. Silhouetted in the foyer of the Beekman Place apartment are the stiff and uncomfortable figures of Norah Muldoon and Patrick, aged 10.

Norah tentatively presses the doorbell. From the interior of the apartment we hear laughter and the muffled gaiety of a fairly well-oiled party. The foyer is decorated in the gaudy Chinoiserie of the late Twenties.

NORAH. (*Looking around uncomfortably.*) It's like the ladies' restroom in the Oriental The-ay-ter.

YOUNG PAT. (*Clutching on to Norah's hand in terror.*) You're not scared, are you, Norah?

NORAH. Of course not, and don't you be, Patrick. Norah's here to look after you. (*She refers to a slip of paper in her trembling hand.*) Number 3, Beekman Place. This is where the lawyer told us to come. We're only doing what he told us. Of course we're not scared, child. (*They are drinking in the strangeness of their surroundings, and do not notice the door as it opens. Ito, a diminutive Japanese houseman, pads out unheard.*)

ITO. You want? (*Norah jumps. Patrick grasps Norah's hand more tightly.*)

NORAH. Glory be to God! I'm Miss . . . that is, I'm Norah Muldoon. And I've been sent by this boy's father—God rest his soul —to bring young Patrick here to live with his aunt, Miss . . . (*She glances again at the slip of paper.*) a Miss Mame Dennis, her name is. (*Ito studies Norah, then young Patrick—still clinging to Norah.*)

ITO. (*With sudden resolve.*) Must be mistake. No want little boy today. (*Ito starts to slam the door, but Norah puts her foot in it.*)

14

NORAH. But I sent the wire from Chicago myself, saying we'd arrive at 6 o'clock today.

ITO. Not important. Boy here, house here, Madam here. You come in. You wait. I fetch. (*Turns.*) Madam having affair now. (*Ito starts to usher them into the noisy interior of the apartment. Young Patrick looks warily at Norah.*)

YOUNG PAT. Norah, do you think we ought to?

NORAH. We've got no choice, Paddy. We've got no place to go. Come, child.

ACT I

SCENE 3

Young Pat and Norah go through the door, and the wall of the foyer breaks away, revealing a cross-section of Mame's Beekman Place apartment. A dozen or more people are milling about at the inebriated apex of a cocktail party. There is apparently a dining room off R. and a bar off L. The guests are continuously crossing back and forth between the hors d'oeuvres and the wet stuff.

Upstage center is a curved staircase which ascends to a bedroom area L.

Norah and Young Pat look about them, baffled by the milling confusion.

GIRL. Oh, Alex, you're simply *murdering* me! (*The apartment is homey as a Shinto shrine—low tables, low sofas, and high guests. Among the guests are a man who looks very much like Alexander Woollcott; a man who looks very much like Robert Benchley; Ralph Devine, a muscular educator; Osbert, a besandaled mystic; an orthodox Lithuanian Bishop; M. Lindsay Woolsey; and other typical cocktail party habitues of the late Twenties. Vera Charles, a famous British actress from Pittsburgh, is holding forth in the center of the room. Ito motions Norah and Pat to a bench, where they sit uncomfortably. There is a cheery panel behind them,*

15

depicting a Japanese nobleman disembowling himself with a Samurai sword. Ito scurries out of sight, in search of Auntie Mame.)

VERA. Mame's been trying to lure me into the daylight for months!—Birds, and the trees and all of that horrible nature business that I can't stand 'til five o'clock in the afternoon.

NORAH. Motheragod, the halls of hell!

RALPH DEVINE. Go on, Vera, go on.

VERA. Well, darling, I couldn't tell you why I ever let Mame persuade me—but Daphne had persuaded Mame that a fling into modern dance would tone her up. And you'll never believe—

RADCLIFFE. *(A He-type She, entering.)* Well, God knows if they want Maude killed professionally, they've sent the poor slob to the right place.

VERA. Radcliffe!

NORAH. White Slavers!

RADCLIFFE. I told her from the start—

VERA. Really, Radcliffe!

RADCLIFFE. Sorry, darling. Didn't realize you were still on.

VERA. Anyway, there we were barefooted, in our camisoles on Daphne's lawn—squatting and unsquatting. Osbert darling, you really should speak to Daphne. Of course, *I* managed beautifully—I was grace personified—but it damned near killed Mame.

OSBERT. Daphne's whole theory of modern dance is based on challenging the pelvis.

VERA. Mame was challenged all right. She had to go to Swami Paramanda for a month to push her pelvis back where it was. *(Lowering her voice.)* Don't, for heaven's sake, mention to Mame that I mentioned this. You know, I adore her, but in a camisole—well!!! *(Mame enters, down the stairs.)*

AUNTIE MAME. I'll get the maid started, Ito. Ring up Bonelli and tell him to get out here with some more gin. *(Auntie Mame's hair is bobbed very short with straight bangs above her slanting brows; a long robe of embroidered golden silk floats out behind her. She wears tiny gold slippers twinkling with jewels, and jade and ivory bracelets clatter on her arms. Her long fingernails are lacquered a delicate green. An almost endless bamboo cigarette holder hangs languidly from her bright red mouth. She crosses*

16

to Norah and looks at her with an expression of bemused surprised.) Oh dear, the Employment Bureau didn't tell me you were bringing a child with you. Well, no matter. He looks like a nice little boy. And if he misbehaves, we can always toss him into the river. (*All laugh, except Norah and Young Pat.*) I guess you know what's expected of you—just a little light slavery around the place.

NORAH. I'm prepared to *buy* my way out. I'll give you my life savings if you'll let this child and me escape from this nest of thieves and slayers! (*Auntie Mame reacts with sad incredulity, then plucks at the sleeve of a distinguished man wearing a goatee.*)

AUNTIE MAME. Dr. Fuchtwanger—just in time. You'd better get this woman on your couch in a hurry.

NORAH. I'm not that kind of a woman, Mum. All I'm looking for is a Miss Mame Dennis who's supposed to live at Number 3, Beekman Place.

AUNTIE MAME. (*Calling.*) Ito, oh, Ito! (*Ito comes on.*) Ito, where here you been? Show this woman the kitchen and get her started on the glasses.

ITO. Oh, Missy Dennis, this not dishwashing lady.

AUNTIE MAME. Oh, I'm so sorry. (*Shrugs.*) Then I must have invited you. What would you like to drink?

NORAH. Did you not get my telegram? I'm Norah Muldoon.

AUNTIE MAME. (*Gasps.*) No! That's not possible. The wire said December first. That's tomorrow. This is November 31st.

NORAH. (*Balefully.*) No, Mum. 'Tis the first, God curse the evil day.

AUNTIE MAME. That's ridiculous. Everyone knows "Thirty days hath September, April, June and Nov". . . Oh, God! (*Dramatically she enfolds Young Pat in her arms.*) But, darling! *I'm* your Auntie *Mame*! (*Baffled, Young Pat submits to Auntie Mame's effusive embrace. She turns toward her guests, lifting her voice.*) Quiet, quiet, everybody. I have an important announcement to make. This is *my little boy.* (*There are reactions of surprise, pleasure and a few raised eyebrows.*) Oh, he's not really *my* little boy. He's my brother's son. From Chicago. (*She sniffs.*) My poor late brother. (*Norah crosses herself. There are some sympathetic clucks and one hiccup.*) This little tyke. In all the whole wide world, I'm his only living relative. And he's my only living relative. (*She stoops down and embraces him again.*) That's all we have, just each other, my little love. (*There are a few moist eyes at this touching scene. Then Mame looks at Young Pat quizzically.*) What's your—(*Recover.*) What am I going to call you, dear?

YOUNG PAT. Pat. Patrick Dennis.

AUNTIE MAME. I know the Dennis part, darling, and from now on you must call me "Auntie Mame." Now, how would you like a mart—? Is it your bedtime? Heavens, it can't be. Do you want the—ah, powder room, darling? Or food? Food, that's it! You must be famished. You run right along in there and help yourself to the caviar—(*Young Pat starts toward the inside room R. She calls after him.*) After that you can go upstairs and read a book or something.

RALPH DEVINE. (*Approaching Mame.*) Oh, Mame! You're not going to let that child *read*? Taste life second hand!

AUNTIE MAME. Ralph, do you think you could work little Patrick into one of your advanced study groups?

RALPH DEVINE. Yes, I think there just might be an opening. (*Young Pat returns from R., munching a deviled egg.*)

AUNTIE MAME. (*To Young Pat.*) Where've you been going to school, dear?

YOUNG PAT. Chicago Boys' Latin.

RALPH DEVINE. (*With a hollow laugh.*) Uh-huh. Where they build a wall of dull encyclopedias around the id!

YOUNG PAT. The id?

RALPH DEVINE. See? Doesn't even know a simple two letter word. That's John Dewey for you.

AUNTIE MAME. (*Explaining to Young Pat.*) Shake hands with Mr. Devine, Patrick. He runs a school down in the Village where they do all sorts of advanced things. Perhaps we'll enroll you there.

YOUNG PAT. (*Eagerly, shaking hands with Ralph.*) Is it a military school? Do they wear uniforms? (*Ralph Devine looks appalled.*)

RALPH DEVINE. In my school, young man, we don't wear *any*-thing.

AUNTIE MAME. It's heaven. (*Norah is shocked, but Ito tugs her out of the room, up the stairs. The party begins to bubble again.*

18

Mame draws Young Pat aside.) Now, these are a lot of your Auntie Mame's most intimate friends; I don't know all their names, but you can just circulate and you'll hear the most fascinating conversation. Oh, I'm sorry you missed the cast of *Blackbirds* but they had to leave early.

YOUNG PAT. Who's he? (*He indicates the bearded patriarch, in mitred cap and jeweled robes, impassively eating stuffed celery.*)

AUNTIE MAME. That's a Lithuanian Bishop. Doesn't speak a word of English. Stimulating man. (*They come into the circle where Vera Charles is holding forth.*) Vera? Vera, this is my little boy. Patrick! I want you to meet a star. One of the great ladies of the theatre, and your Auntie Mame's dearest friend, Vera Charles.

YOUNG PAT. Hello.

VERA. How do you do.

AUNTIE MAME. She just *loves* little boys.

VERA. (*Distastefully.*) Yes. (*Ito helps the Bishop into his cape. Auntie Mame moves toward him.*)

AUNTIE MAME. Oh, Bishop, do you have to run? I'm so sorry. We certainly enjoyed your conversation. Too bad nobody else here spoke Lithuanian. Such a darling—and so worldly for a man of God. (*The Bishop exits* L. *Auntie Mame crosses back to Young Patrick, who had been listening to Vera. Auntie Mame takes his hand and draws the boy away.*) Isn't she scintillating, darling? Now I want you to meet—

YOUNG PAT. Auntie Mame, what's "nymphomania?"

AUNTIE MAME. It's very simple. Nymphomania is—(*Crosses to table, takes out pad and pencil.*) I'll tell you what we're going to do. Everytime you hear a word you don't understand, just take this pad and pencil and write it down. Later on Auntie Mame will explain it to you. (*Young Pat moves to take down words.*) Oh, the adventure of molding a new little life.

OSBERT. Goodbye, Mame, I've got to fly.

AUNTIE MAME. Goodbye, Osbert, darling. I'll see you on Tuesday. Don't catch cold. (*Osbert exits* L. *She notices Young Pat writing.*) Are you enjoying yourself, dear?

YOUNG PAT. I guess so.

AUNTIE MAME. I imagine it's a little confusing—after Chicago and everything.

YOUNG PAT. I guess so, ma'am.

AUNTIE MAME. Uh-uh.

YOUNG PAT. I mean Auntie Mame.

AUNTIE MAME. (*Crosses to Ralph Devine.*) Oh dear, this is tougher than talking with the Lithuanian Bishop. (*Ralph Devine look analytically at Young Pat.*)

RALPH DEVINE. You know why. The poor little fella's a mass of inhibitions. Send him to me. Won't be a repression left after the first semester.

AUNTIE MAME. Consider him enrolled.

RALPH DEVINE. Good. Give his libido a good shaking up, that's what we'll do. Incidentally, Mame, how's *your* libido these days?

AUNTIE MAME. Stirred, but not shaken.

RALPH DEVINE. Who's the lucky man?—still Lindsay Woolsey?

AUNTIE MAME. (*Airily.*) Among others.

RALPH DEVINE. Well, I wouldn't mind being one of the others that he's among.

AUNTIE MAME. You're a naughty boy, Ralph, but you have lovely muscles.

RALPH DEVINE. Well, I don't mean to drink and dash—but I don't want to be late for my rubdown. (*Ralph Devine departs athletically* L. *Vera is carried across in a prone position, with Ito at one end and Lindsay supporting the great actress's feet. Vera is out stone-cold.*)

ITO. Guest room again, Missy?

AUNTIE MAME. No—no, the coats are in there. Dump her in my room. And, Ito, get that God-awful dress off her.

ITO. (*Grinning.*) Me tuck her in. (*He giggles as they carry her up the stairs.*)

YOUNG PAT. Is the English lady dead, Auntie Mame?

AUNTIE MAME. She's not English, darling. She's from Pittsburgh.

YOUNG PAT. She *sounded* English.

AUNTIE MAME. When you're from Pittsburgh, you've got to do something. Now, read me the words you didn't understand.

YOUNG PAT. (*Clearing his throat, reads with difficulty.*) Free-

20

love. Stinko. Hotsy-Totsy Club. Bath-tub gin. Karl Marx. (*He looks up innocently.*) Is he one of the Marx Brothers?

AUNTIE MAME. No, dear.

YOUNG PAT. (*Resuming.*) Narciss-iss-istic. Lys-iss-istrata. Lesbian. Son-of a - - - (*Deftly She rips the pad out of his hands.*)

AUNTIE MAME. My, my, what an eager little mind. (*She rips the page from the pad.*) You won't need some of these words for *months* and months. (*Lindsay Woolsey comes down the stairs.*)

LINDSAY. Well, I suppose the new arrival means you can't have dinner with me tonight.

AUNTIE MAME. You're so understanding, Lindsay.

LINDSAY. Displaced by the younger generation!

AUNTIE MAME. Not at all. Not at all.

LINDSAY. I suppose this means I'll be seeing you even less.

AUNTIE MAME. *More*, Lindsay, more. We'll be taking the little lad to the zoo and the aquarium—and we'll be dropping in your office and you can show him how you publish books. We'll be together almost constantly—the three of us.

LINDSAY. Yeah. That's exactly what I had in mind. (*Lindsay exits* L. *The party is thinning out now. Between leave-takings Auntie Mame tries to make her new little visitor seem at home.*)

AUNTIE MAME. Well, now, there's so much we have to discover about each other. I never had a live little boy around the place before. I did mean to have your bedroom all fixed up for you. A friend of mine is coming in to redo the sculpture room into a nursery—well, it's not really a sculpture room, darling, but a sculptor-friend of mine stayed in it for about six months. Such talented fingers, but what he did to my bust—uh—that's the head you know. Anyway he's going to redo the room for you with bunnies all over everything. (*A Man approaches Auntie Mame. He is supporting a Woman who is completely stoned.*)

MAN. 'Night, Mame. Thanks. (*He extends his hand.*)

AUNTIE MAME. Goodnight, Charles. (*The Girl begins to pass out.*) Watch it, Edna.

MAN. (*As he staggers out* L. *with his companion.*) We're already late for Clifton's party. (*They go.*)

AUNTIE MAME. Give Clifton my love. Tell him I'm sorry to miss it, but to ring me up next week some time. (*To Young Pat.*) Now, let's sit down for one minute and really get to know each other. (*As they sit on bench.*) What did you think of the conversation of the party?

YOUNG PAT. Some of it was a little over my head.

AUNTIE MAME. Good heavens, child, didn't your father ever talk to you?

YOUNG PAT: Hardly ever. I only saw him at breakfast time.

AUNTIE MAME. Well, what did he say then?

YOUNG PAT. He usually said, "Pipe down, kid, the old man's hung."

AUNTIE MAME. Amen. (*Turning to Young Pat.*) What did you do in Chicago for *fun*?

YOUNG PAT. Well, Norah took me to the movies every Saturday afternoon. And I played parchesi with the doorman once in a while—until he got fired.

AUNTIE MAME. Oh dear. Didn't they ever do anything cultural for you in Chicago? (*Waving it away.*) Never mind. (*She pats his cheek.*) Ahhh, your Auntie Mame is going to open doors for you, Patrick—doors you never even dreamed existed! What times we're going to have! (*She rises and crosses to a table up* C., *snapping off the overhead light.*) Now, what on earth did I do with that will? (*Searching through a random stack of papers in the drawer.*) It's here some place. (*Reading from a blue-backed document.*) Five pounds Beluga caviar, get hair done—This can't be it—(*She turns it over.*) Oh, yes, this *is* it. (*Auntie Mame returns to sit beside Young Pat on the bench, and leafs through the legal document.*) Your father says you're to be reared as a Protestant. Well, I've no objection to that. (*She gazes off at the ceiling, drawing on her cigarette.*) Though it would be a shame to deprive you of the exquisite mysteries of the Eastern religions. (*She turns to him.*) Where did you go to church, darling?

YOUNG PAT. The Fourth Presbyterian.

AUNTIE MAME. You mean to say there are *four* Presbyterian churches in a place like Chicago? Well, no matter. I guess we can scrounge around and find some sort of Presbyterian Church in the neighborhood. (*She continues to flip through the document.*) Now there's a lot of fol-de-rol about the Knickerbocker Bank and some Mr. Babcock who's been appointed your trustee. (*She slaps*

22

the will down on her lap, annoyed.) Well, I see what that means. *I* have the responsibility, and your trustee has the authority.

YOUNG PAT. I saw a movie once about a trustee.

AUNTIE MAME. Oh?

YOUNG PAT. There was a big prison break, and the trustee saved the warden's daughter.

AUNTIE MAME. This isn't the kind of a trustee that lives in a prison, dear. As a rule. (*She mouths the name distastefully.*) Mr. Babcock. (*Her nostrils dilate slightly.*) We'll tackle him in our our good time. (*Tosses the will on the floor.*) Now, tell me, Patrick. Is your Auntie Mame anything like you expected?

YOUNG PAT. No, ma'am. The only picture I ever saw of you was with a shawl and a rose between your teeth. Like a Spanish lady. It's in my suitcase that's coming. (*Auntie Mame smiles reminiscently, then seriously*:)

AUNTIE MAME. But didn't your father ever *say* anything—*tell* you anything—about me, before he died?

YOUNG PAT. Yes, ma'am.

AUNTIE MAME. Well, what was it? (*Young Pat gulps.*) Come now, my little love. You must always be perfectly frank with your Auntie Mame.

YOUNG PAT. (*Takes a deep breath, and blurts it out.*) Well, my father said since you're my only living relative, beggars can't be choosers. But to be left in your hands was a fate he wouldn't wish on a *dog!*

AUNTIE MAME. (*Evenly.*) That bastard. (*Dutifully, Young Pat reaches for the pad and starts to write down the strange word. She glances at the boy and speaks sweetly.*) That word, dear, was "Bastard." (*She takes the pad and pencil from Young Pat, and prints in virulent block letters.*) B-A-S-T-A-R-D—(*Magnificently she hands him the pad.*)—And it means *your late father!*

(QUICKLY THE LIGHTS FADE)

ACT I

Scene 4

Scene: Two weeks later. The living room of the apartment, as before, except one panel (not the Hari-Kari one) has been rewallpapered. (In building the sets, these panels should be reversible, or able to slide out easily so that the change is instantaneous.)

A Paperhanger, atop a ladder, is putting some finishing touches on the wild, neocubist wallpaper which he has just hung. He comes down the ladder, looking at his handiwork suspiciously. Norah comes on and makes a little gasp at the sight of the bizarre walls.

NORAH. What is it?

PAPERHANGER. It's wallpaper. But don't look at me. I didn't pick it out, I only pasted it on. Why, is it upside-down?

NORAH. No more than everything else around here, I guess. You haven't seen the boy, have you?

PAPERHANGER. Saw a kid go out 'bout a hour ago.

NORAH. Sendin' him all over the city alone. "He's got to discover New York for himself" says she. "You can't go with him, Norah. We want him to turn out to be independent, don't we?" Independent! He'll turn out to be dead under some truck.

PAPERHANGER. I've got an order here to redo a couple of bedrooms. Can I get in?

NORAH. (*Sarcastically.*) At two o'clock! Why, you'll be lucky to get in by five. She's still sleepin'.

PAPERHANGER. Well, I'll get started in the other bedroom then.

NORAH. Oh, you can't go in there, either!

PAPERHANGER. Why not? She ain't sleeping in two bedrooms, is she?

NORAH. Oh, no. It's the first lady of the American the-ay-ter out cold in the guest room.

PAPERHANGER. Again! What's she do, live here?

NORAH. Miss Charles don't live here. She drinks here and she does her passin' out here. It's a wonder to me their blood hasn't turned to vinegar. Two weeks I've been here and they've had thirteen cocktail parties.

PAPERHANGER. Only thirteen in two weeks!

NORAH. They had to call one off. The bootlegger couldn't come that day. (*Young Pat dashes on, clear across the apron of the stage, and through the door, heading toward the stairs. He carries a model airplane—an approximation of the Spirit of St. Louis.*) Thank God you're safe. (*Pretty fed up with it all, the Paperhanger takes his ladder out* U.C. *back to the kitchen.*)

YOUNG PAT. Where's Auntie Mame? I've got to show her something.

NORAH. (*Going into the kitchen.*) Your Auntie Mame's still asleep. (*She exits out to the kitchen. Young Pat stands at the foot of the stairs and calls up.*)

YOUNG PAT. Auntie Mame! Auntie Mame! (*Auntie Mame appears on the stairway wearing a negligee and a sleeping mask.*)

AUNTIE MAME. (*Confused.*) What is it? What happened?

YOUNG PAT. I've got something to show you. (*Auntie Mame feels her way down the stairs as if it's pitch-black, which it is to her behind her sleeping mask.*) Look! (*Young Pat spins the plane around, which is on a string, attached to a stick. Auntie Mame, half-way down the stairs, lifts her sleeping mask.*)

AUNTIE MAME. My God! Bats! (*Auntie Mame, very hung-over, heads toward the low sofa. Young Pat attempts to show her his new toy, proudly.*)

YOUNG PAT. See? It's got a rubber-band motor, and I whittled the body out of balsa-woods, and—(*Auntie Mame sinks to the couch, gesturing him away, closing her eyes and holding her aching head.*)

AUNTIE MAME. Please, darling—your Auntie Mame's hung. (*Young Pat is deeply hurt by this. It's Chicago all over again. Quietly, he takes the airplane and starts off,* L.)

YOUNG PAT. (*Softly.*) Oh, sure, Auntie Mame. (*Suddenly Auntie Mame realizes what she has done. Peeking through her fingers, she braves the sunlight and calls to the boy.*)

AUNTIE MAME. Patrick. Patrick, come back. (*Young Pat stops at the far side of the room, turns.*) You know, I really am interested in all your projects. But you've got to admit it's a bit surprising for Auntie Mame to find Mr. Lindbergh in her apartment before breakfast. (*She squints at the light.*) Child, how can you *see* with all that light? (*Obligingly, Young Pat crosses downstage and pulls an imaginary venetian blind a hair closed. The lights come down just a mite.*) That's better. Now be a perfect angel and ask Ito to bring me a very light breakfast: black coffee and a sidecar. And you might ask him to fix something for your Aunt Vera. (*Gesturing vaguely upstairs.*) I think I hear her coming to in the guest room. (*Young Pat starts toward the kitchen obediently.*) First—come and give your Auntie Mame a good morning kiss. (*Young Pat starts to run toward her.*) Gently, dear, Gently. (*Young Pat kisses her tenderly on the cheek.*) That was lovely, darling. You'll make some lucky woman very happy some day. (*Gingerly Auntie Mame takes the airplane model and winds the propeller tentatively.*) You know, I really am fascinated by aviation. I never knew before they did it all with rubber bands. (*The telephone on the table alongside the sofa rings insolently. This affects Auntie Mame like a dentist's drill at the nape of her neck. Young Pat picks up the phone.*)

YOUNG PAT. (*Into the phone.*) Hello? Miss Dennis—yes, she's here. Who's calling, please? (*Pause.*) Hold the wire. (*To Auntie Mame, covering the mouthpiece.*) It's Mr. Babcock—from the Knickerbocker Bank. (*Auntie Mame takes the phone, pressing the receiver to her chest.*)

AUNTIE MAME. Oh, my God, I've been dodging him for days. (*Realizing what she's done, she speaks sweetly.*) Oh, hello, Mr. Babcock! How nice to hear your voice at long last. (*Young Pat is attentive, knowing that he is at issue here.*) I, too, am looking forward with anticipation to meeting *you*. (*She listens.*) Oh, the little lad is fine. Just fine. And he, too, can't *wait* to meet you. (*Young Pat shrugs indifferently. Auntie Mame covers the mouthpiece, and speaks hoarsely to Pat.*) Hurry my tray, dear. Auntie needs fuel. (*Young Pat exits to kitchen. Auntie Mame turns back to the phone.*) Please *do* stop by, Mr. Babcock—anytime. (*She goes pale.*) In how many minutes? (*Flustered.*) Yes, Fifty-seventh

Street *is* right in my, uh, "neck-of-the-woods." "Spitting distance." How vivid. (*Pause.*) Come right along. Then you can join me for breakfa—*tea!* (*Nodding.*) Number Three, Beekman Place. Right away. (*She puts down the phone. She lets out a plaintive yell.*) Vera! VERA! Get down here! (*Vera staggers down the stairs, heading for the couch. Vera's evening gown looks as if it had been slept in, which it has. She still wears a totally discouraged orchid. She has one shoe on, and her hair and make-up are a mess.*)

VERA. (*Wobbly and incoherent.*) Did you call me, darling?

AUNTIE MAME. (*Getting up.*) I'm about to be attacked by the Knickerbocker Bank.

VERA. (*Falling onto the couch.*) That's lovely. Why in hell did that Japanese sandman let me sleep in my best Lanvin?

AUNTIE MAME. He tried to get it off you, but you bit him. Patrick's trustee is on his way over here.

VERA. It's ruined. Absolutely ruined.

AUNTIE MAME. Some hideous creature who's coming here to thwart all the plans I've made for the boy's cultural enlargement!

VERA. (*Incredulously.*) He's coming here—in the middle of the night? (*Vera, half rising, blinks at the partially opened blinds.*) My God, that moon's bright. (*She falls right back down again.*)

AUNTIE MAME. Oh, don't be silly, Vera. Don't you realize— some horrible man is descending like a vulture to rob me of my child?

VERA. Mame, you're being *utterly* hysterical.

AUNTIE MAME. I've got to make the right impression. You have no idea how conservative the Knickerbocker Bank is; it's so conservative they don't pay any interest at *all*. (*Vera rises, hazily, slapping herself in the face to waken herself. Auntie Mame goes to the kitchen door and shouts out to Norah.*) Norah, find me a dress I can wear—quick. Bring down a whole stack. And in my dressing-table drawer, there is a box of hair. I've got to do something to my head. (*Norah scampers out from kitchen through the above and mounts the stairs, dutily but doubtfully.*)

VERA. All right. Let's get organized. What time is it? What *day* is it? (*Vera picks up a clock and looks at it in horror.*) Blessed

27

mother of Maude Adams. I was due at the Theatre Guild an hour ago.

AUNTIE MAME. You can't desert me in my predicament, Vera. Look at my face. What on earth am I going to wear?

VERA. How am I going to face the Theatre Guild? The way I look I couldn't even understudy a witch in "Macbeth."

AUNTIE MAME. (*Hurrying to the foot of the stairs.*) That's just like you, Vera! Here my life is about to be blown to bits—and all you can think of is your career! (*Norah comes down the stairs, carrying a large stack of multi-colored dresses. On top is a cardboard box, covered.*) Thank you, Norah. (*Mame takes off the top dress and holds it against herself. It is a flashy red dress, with beads, sequins, and spangles.*) Will this make me look like a Scarsdale matron? (*Vera squints at her, disbelieving.*)

VERA. Have you ever *been* to Scarsdale? (*Young Pat enters from the kitchen with a small breakfast tray on which there are a cup of coffee and a side-car.*)

YOUNG PAT. Good afternoon, Auntie Vera.

VERA. Yes, dear. (*Vera takes the side-car and pours it straight down.*) Do the Jane Cowl routine. You know, conservative dress, madonna-like hair do.

AUNTIE MAME. Madonna-like hair-do. That's it. A switch. A switch.

VERA. Have you got one?

AUNTIE MAME. (*Taking the box from Norah and uncovering it.*) Dozens. (*She pulls out an array of switches, that puts a rainbow to shame.*)

VERA. My God, don't you ever throw anything away?

AUNTIE MAME. Who knows when I may go back to one of these colors?

VERA. If you kept your hair natural the way I do, you wouldn't need—

AUNTIE MAME. If I kept my hair natural the way you do, I'd be bald. Pick out the one nearest to mine.

VERA. (*Picking out the black one and tossing it on the couch.*) Try this. And you need a dress—like the one I wore when I played Lady Esme in "Summer Folly." (*Mame takes a lovely green frock from the pile on Norah's arms.*) Oh, that's stunning.

28

AUNTIE MAME. Isn't it? It's my new Maggie Rouf. But I've never had it on yet. And I'll be damned if I'll put five hundred dollars on my back for that awful man. (*An idea.*) A suit! A suit! That'll do. (*Picks up the switch.*) Help me braid this switch so it looks like a halo.

VERA. (*Protesting.*) I've got to get over to the Guild!

AUNTIE MAME. Vera, you can't desert me! (*Vera helps Auntie Mame reluctantly.*)

VERA. *You* should be helping *me*. Do you want me to *lose* this part? (*Vera is braiding Auntie Mame's switch furiously then drops it. Auntie Mame puts one end of the switch in her mouth and braids it herself.*) It's this lovely, lovely play where every-body thinks out loud and it runs four-and-a-half hours. It's called "Strange—" (*She can't remember the title, and gropes for it.*) Strange Inter—Inter—Inter"

AUNTIE MAME. (*Helpfully.*) "Course?"

VERA. For God's sake, no. They're opening in Boston. I do hope Lawrence and Terry don't think I'm too British for the part. They'll probably give it to that Lynn what's-her-name.

AUNTIE MAME. Ouch! (*Mr. Babcock appears* D.L. *in the foyer and rings the door buzzer.*) Not already! (*Calls.*) Ito,—answer the door!

VERA. I've got to get out before he gets in!

AUNTIE MAME. Well, I can't leave him standing in the foyer like a Fuller Brush man.

VERA. What do you want me to do, fly out the chimney?

AUNTIE MAME. Oh, Vera, for heaven's sake—

VERA. (*Grandly.*) You can't expect me to appear before my public looking as if I'd been slept in!

AUNTIE MAME. Really, Vera—one banker doesn't make a mati-nee. (*Pinning the braid hastily.*) All right. Wait upstairs, I'll get rid of him in five minutes—I promise.

VERA. Mame, you just don't understand the responsibility of being in the public eye. (*Babcock, in the foyer, is getting impa-tient. He presses the door buzzer again. Auntie Mame starts to-ward the stairs and her braid topples into her face.*)

AUNTIE MAME. Norah, get all this junk back upstairs. (*Norah gathers the dresses together rather frantically, but drops a frizzy*

29

negligee on the floor, the hanger still in it. Norah goes up the stairs, shaking her head at this mad-house. Auntie Mame turns urgently to Young Pat.) Patrick. Make Mr. Babcock feel right at home, just like Auntie Mame taught you.

YOUNG PAT. Sure, Auntie Mame. *(Auntie Mame pushes Vera up the stairs with a shove in the derriere.)*

VERA. *(Protesting.)* But the Theatre Guild.

AUNTIE MAME. *(The other hand is struggling with the switch.)* What am I going to do with this *God* damned halo????? *(Babcock is punching the door-buzzer a little irritably. Young Pat looks frantically for a place to deposit the breakfast tray, finally goes into the kitchen with it. Ito emerges from kitchen, crossing him, and going toward the door. En route, he sees the negligee on the floor. Used to this madness, he calmly picks it up and has it in his raised hand as he crosses L. and opens the door for Babcock.)*

ITO. You want?

BABCOCK. Babcock is the name. Miss Dennis is expecting me.

ITO. Okay. You come in. *(Babcock is conservative to the very inlays of his molars, with all the personality of steam-roller wearing a vest.)* I take coat. *(Ito starts to help Babcock off with his coat, but cannot manage it while carrying the negligee. He gives the negligee to Babcock who holds it awkwardly. Ito starts off R. with Babcock's coat and muffler, leaving the banker holding the negligee.)* You sit.

BABCOCK. Say—! *(Ito takes the negligee from the slightly ruffled Babcock, and scampers off giggling. Young Pat enters from the kitchen and greets Mr. Babcock with unaffected composure.)*

YOUNG PAT. Mr. Babcock?

BABCOCK. That's right, Sonny.

YOUNG PAT. We've been expecting you. *(He offers his hand.)* My name is Patrick Dennis.

BABCOCK. *(Shaking the boy's hand.)* Fine, fine.

YOUNG PAT. Please sit down, Mr. Babcock. My Auntie Mame will be right down. She's having trouble with her halo. *(Recovers.)* She'll be right down.

BABCOCK. Fine, fine. *(They look at each other, realizing they*

30

have absolutely nothing to communicate.) Well, you look like a bully little chap. Yes, sir, a bully little chap.

YOUNG PAT. You look very bully, too, Mr. Babcock.

BABCOCK. (*Clears his throat.*) Yes. Well, you seem to be taking all this like a regular little soldier. Oh, say, I have a boy just about your age up in Darien. We'll have you up soon, and Junior can show you his cigar-band collection.

YOUNG PAT. (*Politely.*) That would be swell. (*Babcock slaps his knees and rises impatiently.*) Would you care for a martini, Mr. Babcock?

BABCOCK. No, thank you. (*He breaks off, startled, as he sees the hari-kari painting.*) Maybe you'd better order me one, Sonny.

YOUNG PAT. (*Wheeling the portable bar toward* R.C.) Dry or extra dry? (*Babcock is about to reply, but stops open-mouthed to watch Young Pat as he takes a Martini glass with great finesse, breathes in it and dries it snappily with a cocktail towel. The boy holds the glass up to the light and squints through it approvingly.*) Please sit down. (*Babcock's mouth has sprung open, and apparently he's not going to reply.*) I'll make 'em like I do for Mr. Woollcott. (*From an ice bucket, he drops some cubes into a pitcher; then he pours in a great quantity of gin and stirs.*) Stir —never shake. Bruises the gin. (*Babcock nods mechanically. Young Pat uncorks the vermouth, pours a smidgeon into the glass, swills it around by rotating the stem then empties it completely.*) Would you care for an olive? Auntie Mame says olives take up too much room in such a little glass! (*Babcock shakes his head, his jowls flapping, and takes the glass. The Banker takes one sip, then turns to see Auntie Mame coming down the stairs demurely—complete with braided coronet and all the aplomb of a Scarsdale matron being played by Jane Cowl. She blanches at Young Pat's alcoholic gambit, but makes a lightning recovery. Young Pat wheels the bar back into place.*)

AUNTIE MAME. (*Grandly.*) Why, Mr. Babcock, what an honor it is to have you in our little home. (*She draws him aside, confidentially.*) Though I wonder if it makes the best first impression on a sensitive young mind to see you drinking during business hours.

BABCOCK. (*Floundering indignantly.*) But—but *he*—

31

AUNTIE MAME. (*Patting his arm reassuringly.*) Don't you worry, I won't breathe a word to the Knickerbocker Bank. (*Babcock puts down the drink on table, and tries to slide it out of sight, behind him. He can't quite figure out how he has been put on the defensive.*)

BABCOCK. Now, just a minute. Where did that youngster learn to mix a—

AUNTIE MAME. (*With dignified hauteur.*) Mr. Babcock. Knowledge is power! (*This stops him.*)

BABCOCK. (*Clears his throat.*) That, Miss Dennis, is exactly what I am here for. To discuss this youngster's education. His *proper* education.

AUNTIE MAME. (*Offering a dish.*) Nuts?

BABCOCK. No, thank you.

AUNTIE MAME. *Do* sit down, Mr. Babcock. (*They do. Mr. Babcock finds himself uncomfortably close to the floor on the Japanese settee. Auntie Mame sits opposite him, and Young Pat sits on the ottoman between them. He looks back and forth from one speaker to the other as his fate is being decided.*)

BABCOCK. (*Very business-like.*) Now. All the money this little fella's "Dad" left him is in good, steady bonds. So he never has to worry where his next meal is coming from. Unless—um—the Bolshevikis take over the government. Or the Democrats get back in.

AUNTIE MAME. Jelly beans?

BABCOCK (*Taking one.*) Now I'm sure you agree that it's high time this little shaver was enrolled in some institution of learning.

YOUNG PAT. (*Brightly.*) Oh, I'm already—

AUNTIE MAME. Now—now. Let Mr. Babcock talk, dear.

BABCOCK. Now. I've gone to, uh, some pains to, uh, gather information on a number of the better boys' schools in town. (*He brings list from inside coat pocket.*)

AUNTIE MAME. Personally, I prefer co-educational schools.

BABCOCK. (*Shocked.*) What do you mean?

YOUNG PAT. (*Helpfully.*) Co-educational means when boys and girls go—

BABCOCK. I know. I know. (*Clears his throat.*) First on my list is the Buckley School, which is known to be splendid.

AUNTIE MAME. Have you considered a school down in the village run by a Mr. Ralph Devine? It's wonderfully progressive and—

BABCOCK. (*Holding up a hand as if directing rush-hour traffic.*) Your late brother was very specific in his will. He said *conservative* schooling. (*Consulting his list.*) Now, the Browning School gives a boy the basics. Three years of Latin—(*While Babcock is speaking, Vera appears at the top of the stairs behind him. She gesticulates vigorously to Mame, who is facing her. Babcock looks up.*)

AUNTIE MAME. (*Covering.*) That's enough candy, dear. Not you, Mr. Babcock. Have as much as you like. (*Quickly.*) Have you thought of the Dalton School? It's right up—

BABCOCK. No, no. That one is a *little* too experimental. (*He digs out several pamphlets.*) We must choose a school which is both exclusive and restricted.

AUNTIE MAME. (*Gritting her teeth.*) Exclusively *what* and restricted to *whom?*

BABCOCK. Want to keep the riffraff out of this lad's life—(*Mame is about to explode.*)

AUNTIE MAME. Mr. Babbitt—

BABCOCK. Babcock.

AUNTIE MAME. Yes. Uh—exactly who decides which is riff and which is raff?

BABCOCK. Now, Miss Dennis, unless we can agree on some proper school here in Manhattan, we shall have to consider an institution such as *my* alma mater, St. Boniface, up in Massachusetts.

AUNTIE MAME. No, no, that's too far away! Have you thought of the Ethical Culture School—that's just across town?

BABCOCK. I'd like to keep that west-side influence out of the boy's life as much as possible. (*Auntie Mame stands, icily, indicating that the interview is over.*)

AUNTIE MAME. It was very good of you to come, Mr. Babcock.

BABCOCK. But we haven't arrived at any conclusions.

AUNTIE MAME. Haven't we?

BABCOCK. Well, what school is it going to be?

AUNTIE MAME. You name the school of your choice, and Patrick and I will know exactly what to do.

BABCOCK. (*Strongly.*) I'd say Buckley.

AUNTIE MAME. Then *bully* for Buckley.

BABCOCK. Well—(*This was easier than he thought it would be.*) For a minute there, I thought we were going to have a little friction. (*He chortles.*) But I'm glad to see you're actually a fine, sensible woman. I'll make out a check to the Buckley School and you can take him down and register him.

AUNTIE MAME. (*Sweetly.*) Whatever you say. Well, it's so nice of you to—(*Vera, with a scarf tied around her head like a peasant babuchka, comes down stairs and plods across the room. She is wearing Auntie Mame's new Maggie Rouf and dragging Auntie Mame's best mink on the floor behind her.*)

VERA. (*In a thick accent.*) Floor all scrubbed, Fraulein Dennis. Clean yoost like in old country. I go now, get lamb chops, two bottles milk for boy.

AUNTIE MAME. (*Between her teeth.*) Pick up my coat.

YOUNG PAT. Goodbye, Auntie Vera.

VERA. (*Back in her own voice.*) 'Bye, kid. (*There is a big take from the already bewildered Babcock, as Vera scoots out the front door, on her way to the Theatre Guild. Auntie Mame turns innocently back to Babcock.*)

AUNTIE MAME. You were saying, Mr. Babcock?

THE LIGHTS FADE

ACT I

SCENE 5

The panels of the living room have been switched and the furnishings have been redressed, as much as time will allow. The wall-paper is now modern.

The phone rings. The Paperhanger is coming down his ladder, looks around at his handiwork, shakes his head. Ito enters from the foyer D.R., carrying a chart.

PAPERHANGER. Phone's ringin'. (*He goes out* U.C. *to kitchen. Ito puts down the chart on table, facing upstage, and picks up the phone.*)

ITO. (*Into phone.*) Missy Dennis residence. Stock Broker? Missy Dennis not here, you call back next month some time. (*He listens.*) Missy Dennis say anybody who call servant dirty bastard is dirty bastard. (*He puts down the phone, smiling happily. Norah enters* D.L. *in a hat and coat, her arms full of groceries.*)

NORAH. (*To Ito.*) Now, where've *you* been?

ITO. Missy Dennis send me 'cross ocean. Staten Island. Bring back body.

NORAH. What body?

ITO. For boy.

NORAH. (*Reading cover on chart.*) "The Physiological Anatomical Medical Supply Company." What in the name of St. Brigid is it?

ITO. Missy say boy gotta know inside like outside. (*He flips over the cover, revealing a skeleton.*)

NORAH. Oh, the poor man. Nothin' but a liver, God rest his soul. (*She crosses herself.*)

ITO. (*Starting up stairs with chart.*) Missy say put in boy's room.

NORAH. I dare ya. There's not an inch of space left up there.

ITO. I make space. I put white mice your room. (*He giggles.*)

NORAH. (*As she goes into kitchen.*) Put 'em in your own pagoda, ya heathen! (*Auntie Mame and Lindsay come in the foyer. They are loaded down with packages and boxes. Auntie Mame is aglow with excitement and decked out in furs, but Lindsay is getting a little tired of this maternal bit. They come into the apartment.*)

AUNTIE MAME. What a day! What a lovely, lovely day!

LINDSAY. What a day is right. On our feet for five hours—no lunch. Why don't they put a bar in F.A.O. Schwartz? I haven't even had a chance to call my office. I might have been bought out by Knopf.

AUNTIE MAME. Stop complaining, Lindsay. Fix yourself a drink. And then we can open the parcels. I can't wait to see Patrick's face when he sees all these lovely things.

LINDSAY. Mame! When are we going to have a day, an hour, a minute—some time to ourselves?

35

AUNTIE MAME. Time! Lindsay, don't you realize I've had to make up for Patrick's ten neglected years in a matter of months. (*Picking up a brightly colored book.*) Dr. Giselle says it's practically an impossibility.

LINDSAY. Does Dr. Giselle also happen to mention that what a child needs is a father?

AUNTIE MAME. Now, Lindsay—

LINDSAY. (*Pressing on.*) You know there are a lot of women in this town who think I'm a reasonably good catch. I'm reasonably successful; you've admitted yourself that I'm reasonably attractive, I'm reasonably . . .

AUNTIE MAME. Oh, Lindsay, that's the trouble. You're "reasonably" everything. You're reasonably in love with me, and we'd be reasonably happy. But that's not enough. Besides how can I be a wife? I'm too busy being a mother. (*The door bell buzzes.*)

LINDSAY. There was Coue, Dada, Nature Foods, modern dance—

AUNTIE MAME. Oh, you think Patrick is a *phase*—

LINDSAY. Well, frankly, I do. (*Babcock bursts in from* D.L.)

BABCOCK. Where is she? Where is that mad-woman? Where is that irresponsible, deceitful Bohemian Delilah? (*Lindsay tries to protest, through the entire following scene—but never succeeds in getting more than a word in edgewise.*)

LINDSAY. Now just a minute, Sir—

AUNTIE MAME (*With a hollow hauteur.*) Why, Mr. Babcock, whatever do you mean?

BABCOCK. You know damned well what I mean. Why, you're no more fit to raise a child than Jezebel! (*Auntie Mame, concerned, rushes forward.*)

AUNTIE MAME. Patrick! Something's happened to my little love!

BABCOCK. You're damn right someth—Come in here, you little heathen! (*He drags Young Pat into the room from* D.L. *Young Pat huddles in an overcoat, with apparently nothing on underneath.*)

AUNTIE MAME. Patrick—what's wrong? (*Before the boy can answer, Babcock thunders on.*)

PATRICK. Well, he came over to my school—

BABCOCK. I'll tell you what's wrong. I was doing my conscientious duty. I dropped by the Buckley School to check on the kid's

36

academic standing. And what did I find? He isn't even registered. Never has been. So I've been hunting in every low, half-baked school for the feeble-minded in this town. And finally I found him—in the lowest of them all.

AUNTIE MAME. Mr. Devine is a progressive educator. He uses the same theory as Bertrand Russell does in England—

BABCOCK. I walk into that so-called "institution of learning"— and what do I find? A whole school-room of 'em—boys, girls, teachers—romping around, stark naked! Bare as the day they were born!

AUNTIE MAME. I can assure you that the students under Mr. Devine's care were engaged in healthful, broadening pursuits.

BABCOCK. Broadening. (*Turns to Young Pat.*) Show 'em what you were doing when I broke into the place. Go ahead—show 'em!

YOUNG PAT. We were just playing fish families.

BABCOCK. "Fish families!"

YOUNG PAT. It's part of constructive play.

BABCOCK. Listen to this.

AUNTIE MAME. Show me, darling.

YOUNG PAT. Well, we do it just after Yogurt Time. Mrs. Devine and all the girls crouch down on the floor under the sun lamps— and they pretend to be lady fishes, depositing their eggs in the sand. Then Mr. Devine and all the boys do what gentlemen fish do.

AUNTIE MAME. What could be more wholesome or natural?

BABCOCK. Natural! It might be natural for a sardine! (*To Lindsay.*) Would you put a boy of yours in a school like that?

AUNTIE MAME. Mr. Babcock. I consider your behavior most undignified.

BABCOCK. Undignified! At least I'm wearing a vest.

AUNTIE MAME. Making a scene. Causing what might well be a traumatic experience for this child.

BABCOCK. (*Holding up a hand.*) Look, I know how you can twist things around. So I'm getting out of this combination nudist-camp-opium-den, before you make *me* look like the vice-president in charge of free love!

AUNTIE MAME. (*Righteously covering Pat's ears.*) Mr. Babcock. Not in front of the B-O-Y! (*Babcock goes toward the* D.L. *exit, turns threateningly.*)

BABCOCK. Tomorrow morning, I, me, *personally*—I'm taking this kid off to boarding school myself. I'm placing him in St. Boniface Academy and he's going to stay there. The only time you'll get your depraved hands on him is Christmas and summer and I wish to God there was some way to prevent that.

YOUNG PAT (*Running to Auntie Mame.*) Auntie Mame. Do I have to? Do I?

AUNTIE MAME. (*Frantically.*) Please, Mr. Babcock—I'll do whatever you say. If you'll only let the child stay near me.

BABCOCK. Not on your life! He goes, and he goes tomorrow.

LINDSAY. Now let's be reasonable about this—

BABCOCK. I'm going to turn this kid into a decent, God-fearing Christian if I have to break every bone in his body.

AUNTIE MAME. If you'll give me another chance—

BABCOCK. I wouldn't give you the time of day, after the dirty doublecross you pulled on me.

AUNTIE MAME. (*Pleading in real desperation.*) Mr. Babcock, he's all I have, he's my life.

BABCOCK. You have him ready by 8 o'clock *sharp.* And, kid, you'd better be wearing knickers! (*He exits* L.)

YOUNG PAT. I want to stay with you, Auntie Mame. I don't want to go to that old St. Bony Face.

AUNTIE MAME. Hush, my little love. I'm sure St. Boniface is really very nice. Now, go upstairs and get ready for dinner and we'll talk about it later. (*She watches as Pat climbs the stairs.*) Lindsay, Lindsay. What am I going to do?

LINDSAY. (*Honestly concerned.*) Don't worry, Mame. I'll help you. I'll get the kid back some way.

AUNTIE MAME. (*Crying.*) I just don't think I can bear it. I just don't—

LINDSAY. Mame, I've never seen you cry before . . . (*Lindsay tries to comfort her. The doorbell jabs insistently and we hear the strident voice of Vera in the outside hall.*)

VERA. (*From off.*) Mame, are you in there?

AUNTIE MAME. Oh, I just couldn't take anything else today!

VERA. It's urgent, it's vital, it's *dire!* (*She hurries on stage.*) Have you talked to your stock broker? (*She looks at the unhappy Mame.*) Yes. I can see you have.

LINDSAY. What about her stock broker?

VERA. Don't you know? He's called me half a dozen times, trying to locate both of you.

LINDSAY. (*Paling slightly.*) What happened?

VERA. Oh, nothing—except that nothing's worth anything any more! (*Phone rings.*)

LINDSAY. Don't you worry, Mame. I'm sure this is only something temporary. It can't possibly affect people like you and me—who have a lot of solid stuff like Bank of the United States. (*Ito scampers in from kitchen to answer the phone. He covers the mouthpiece, then speaks blandly to Auntie Mame.*)

ITO. Missy Dennis. Stock broker want to say hello before he jump out of window. (*Lindsay grabs phone.*)

LINDSAY. (*Into phone.*) How bad is it, Arthur? (*The blood drains from his face.*) Everything? (*He can hardly say it.*) At-water-Kent, too???????? (*Slowly he puts down the telephone, stunned.*) Mame, I'm afraid you're wiped out. We *all* are.

VERA. (*Philosophically.*) And everybody said I was such a fool, spending all my money at Tiffany's.

AUNTIE MAME. Who gives a damn about money? I've lost my child.

VERA. What?

LINDSAY. Patrick's trustee is sending him away to school.

VERA. Oh, Mame, darling—I know how you must feel.

AUNTIE MAME. Do you?

VERA. Well, not exactly, of course. I've never *had* a child. But, after all, I'm an actress, I can imagine. (*Abruptly, business-like.*) Now look—I've got everything worked out for you—I've got the perfect solution for all your problems. I'm going to tell Brock he simply *has* to give you a part in my new play. It opens Thanksgiving in New Haven.

AUNTIE MAME. No, thanks, Vera, I don't want your charity, I don't want anything but—

VERA. No, no, darling. It isn't charity, I want you in it. Besides, Patrick's trustee is sure to let Patrick come back when he finds out you've settled down into something steady like acting.

AUNTIE MAME. Do you really think so, Vera?

VERA. Oh, I know he would. Don't you agree, Lindsay?

LINDSAY. Well—

AUNTIE MAME. Oh, but you're so right, Vera. And if he didn't, I'd be earning the money to fight him. About $500 a week to start, don't you think? And then they'll be a raise—

VERA. Mame, it'll only be a bit—at the end of the last act. (*Persuasively*.) But it'll be like old times! Think of the fun we had trouping together in "Chu-Chin-Chow."

AUNTIE MAME. I accept, I accept. Vera, your heart is from Tiffany's too. Oh, I can't wait to hear the overture!

VERA. Mame—this is a drama. Serious drama. I play the part of a Balkan Princess who—

MAME. (*To Lindsay*.) I was in the front line of the chorus and Vera was behind me.

VERA. Behind you! If I'd been behind you, I'd have kicked you in the behind, you.

AUNTIE MAME. (*Sings illustratively*).
>   "I'm a Chu Chu Girl from Chu-Chin-Chow.
>   And how!"

(*Clicks tongue*.)
>   "And how!"

(*Clicks tongue*.)

VERA. (*Pushes Mame into the back row*.) "I'd love to chin and chew with you.

AUNTIE MAME. (*With elaborate gestures*.) And turn the skies to blue with you.

VERA (*Showing her how it was really done*.) And turn the skies to blue with you.

AUNTIE MAME. That's it!

BOTH. (*Harmonizing*.)
>   And twenty-three skidoo with you!
>   Chee-chee! Choo-Choo! Chow-Chow!

(*Click tongues*.)
>   And how!

(*Click tongues*.)
>   And how! And how!"

(*Hilariously they fall into each other's arms. Mercifully the lights fade on the two Sing-Song Girls*.)

ACT I

SCENE 6

SCENE: *The stage of the Shubert Theatre, New Haven. Reverse angle.*

Note: in the New York production, there was a drop that was lowered, showing the back-side of a set, plus an actual working curtain. As it rose, we saw balcony lights, as if shining toward the actors. It is suggested for a simplified production, that a row of portable foot-lights be carried on in the darkness and placed against the back drop or traveller. As curtain rising or lowering is indicated, these multi-colored foots—angling up into the actors' faces—can be brought up or brought down.

This row of spots can be carried on in the darkness, as we hear the Stage-manager's voice.

It is suggested, that in lieu of the back-side of the sets, several screens be carried on, behind which the offstage action can be played.

STAGE MANAGER. Set up for Act Three, Scene Two. And quiet on stage. There are still critics out there—I hope.

MAID. (*Off.*) I can't find my feather duster.

STAGE MANAGER. Props! Get 'em their feather dusters. Lemme have a work light, Bob. (*The work-light comes on. The Theatre Manager rushes back-stage. He is a splenetic man with glasses and a cigar, bred by the Shuberts.*)

THEATRE MANAGER. (*Pointing up-stage to the theatre audience behind the house curtain.*) Look, half the audience out there has gone home, and the other half has gone to sleep. Does this play ever *end*????

STAGE MANAGER. We're almost set, Mr. Unger. (*The Assistant Stage Manager comes out with a prop-bench. Norah hurries on.*)

NORAH. Miss Dennis ain't ready.

THEATRE MANAGER. Who the hell is Miss Dennis?

STAGE MANAGER. She plays Lady Iris.

THEATRE MANAGER. That's a two-line bit.

STAGE MANAGER. Shh—!

NORAH. (*Starting off.*) She wants more time to arrange her accessories.

STAGE MANAGER. (*Exploding.*) She's had two and a half acts to arrange her damned accessories.

THEATRE MANAGER. Get that curtain up—and if that Dennis dame ain't ready—(*He clamps the cigar in his teeth.*)—*I'll* play Lady Iris.

STAGE MANAGER. Lights. Kill the work light. Take it up, Bob. (*The audience for this play-within-a-play is presumed to be at extreme up-stage. The worklight goes off. The curtain, up-stage, rises and we see footlights shining directly into our faces. The business of the play, therefore, is directed upstage; but the asides in the following are given downstage, to the actual theatre audience. The Maid and Butler dust furiously. Everything that he dusts, she dusts again immediately afterwards.*)

MAID. What do you suppose is happening now, Meadows, in the conservatory?

BUTLER. It is all over, Perkins. It is done with! We have lost the master—and, worse than that, the master has lost himself.

MAID. But love burns bright in this house tonight, Meadows!

BUTLER. And we shall all be consumed in the flames!

MAID. Don't be ridiculous, Meadows. Tonight we are living a legend. There is a *princess* beneath this roof, and every room vibrates with the fragrance of this fragile royal flower!

BUTLER. And our master is drugged by the heady perfume.

MAID. (*Quickly, resuming her dusting.*) Hush, Meadows. They are coming now! (*The Maid and Butler scurry off. From the opposite side, Vera and her Leading Man enter dramatically. Vera is svelte and statuesque, and her Leading Man is more of a matinee idol than is absolutely necessary. He always seems about to speak, but never manages to get a line out—Vera has seen to that; she also does a polished job of upstaging the poor guy.*)

VERA. But, Rrrreginald, tew dew sech a thing—tew desh oaf tewgethaw lake thisss—would be med; quate enchantingly med.

(*Auntie Mame comes into the wings in flaming red. Norah is helping her as she does last minute primping. On her wrists are clanging bell bracelets. An uncomfortable actor in tails stands alongside of Mame. He plays the part of Lord Dudley.*)

AUNTIE MAME. Oooooooh, Lord Dudley. Your flahterry is enough to turn a young girl's head! (*There is the tinkling of bells. Vera touches her coiffeur, and begins again.*)

VERA. Naow, Rreginald, it would be medness. Ay belung tew one wuld, yew tew anothah. It's bettah thet we paht now; now whale we cheddish this ecstasy we've known. (*Vera moves regally toward the wings, then speaking away from her audience, but so we can hear clearly, she drops all affectation and speaks in good clear Pittsburgh.*) What the hell have you got back there—reindeer? (*She wheels upstage toward her own audience and instantaneously resumes her Mayfair elegance.*) This is gudbay, Rreginald. Ay heah the othahs coming. (*The Others sweep on, led by Auntie Mame on the arm of an embarrassed stage Lord. Around her wrists are the bracelets, we have seen—and heard—before: fashioned from large silver Siamese temple bells. With very gesture, she drowns out the dialogue. Vera glares at her with all the loving kindness of the Apache Kid on the warpath.*)

AUNTIE MAME. (*As she enters; with an uninhibited stage laugh.*) Ooooooh, no mahr champagne, Lord Dudleh, or I shall forget myself altogethah! (*She makes a sweeping gesture and the bells clang like New Year's Eve.*)

VERA. (*Frigidly poking Mame in the back with her elbow.*) Ay've sumthing tew tale yew ull. Ay'm nut gaowing to meddy Rrrreginald after ull. May place is at haome with Prince Alexiss. Ay must gaow beck—beck to may wuld. (*Reginald looks crushed. Auntie Mame, on a sudden Stanislawsky impulse, pats his arm comfortingly. The effect is as subtle as the passing of a fire-engine. Reginald steps out of reach. Vera turns to Auntie Mame, with a look that would paralyze the average Bengal tiger.*) Lady Irrriss. Would yew be gude enough to rrring for my wrrrap!

AUNTIE MAME. Certainly, Princess. (*She curtseys deeply; the bells peal deafeningly. A Footman hands Auntie Mame the wrap, folded. It is a voluminous chinchilla. As Auntie Mame advances to Vera, Vera turns toward us and mutters menacingly.*)

43

VERA. And get rid of those goddamn cow-bells! (*Flustered, Auntie Mame tries to muffle the bells in the coat as Vera turns with a gracious wave toward her audience.*)

AUNTIE MAME. Do let me help you, Princess. (*She puts the cape over Vera's shoulders upside-down, the hem at her neck, the collar sweeping the floor.*)

VERA. Thank yew, Lady Iris. (*An awful look comes over her face as she realizes the cape is upside down. She points down her back to the collar. Auntie Mame engages in a brief but unsuccessful battle with the chinchilla. Vera decides to get off and quick.*) Gudbay, gudbay. I shall always feel a deep attechment for you ull! (*As Vera sweeps off, Auntie Mame's outstretched hand mysteriously remains connected to the small of Vera's back, so that she is tugged along toward the exit. The bells keep clanging. Vera grunts, over her shoulder.*) Let go. For God's sake, *let go*!

AUNTIE MAME. (*Helplessly wailing.*) I can't let go. I'm caught. I'm stuck! (*There is some less-than-amiable thrashing as the two women try to disentangle themselves.*)

STAGE MANAGER'S VOICE. (*Off, frantic.*) Curtain! Bring down the curtain! (*There is the anaesthetic lowering of velour, cutting off the ribald laughter and cat-calls.*) Places for curtain calls! (*The Actors make a formal line facing upstage, but Auntie Mame is still enmeshed with Vera.*)

VERA. You amateur! (*The curtain rises, and All bow graciously to the audience upstage. The curtain comes down.*)

AUNTIE MAME. (*Miserable.*) I was only trying—

VERA. Ruining my beautiful play with your goddam Swiss-bell-ringing act!

AUNTIE MAME. But, Vera, they're the only bracelets I have left—(*The curtain goes up again for a second curtain time. More bows. Vera flings off the encumbrance of the Chinchilla and Auntie Mame. She does this with such violence that Auntie Mame is catapulted forward into what seems to be a solo curtain call. The applause is thunderous.*)

VERA. That's enough! (*The curtain falls again. The Stage Manager comes on, wild-eyed.*)

STAGE MANAGER. That's enough! Strike the set! Work-light!

VERA. (*Wheeling on Mame.*) Why did you do this to me? Why?
AUNTIE MAME. (*Honestly distraught.*) I was only trying to *make* something out of Lady Iris—give her some character . . .
VERA. You scene-stealing society bitch! (*Turns her back on Auntie Mame.*) Oh, God. And there were Critics out there. We're ruined. We're all ruined. (*As she goes off.*) Ruined. Ruined. (*She's gone. The others in the cast avoid Auntie Mame as if she had a touch of leprosy.*)
AUNTIE MAME. I was only trying to—I was only—(*They're all gone now—and just the bare work-lights and a box remain on the empty stage. Auntie Mame sinks down, alone and dismal. Young Pat comes hesitantly toward Auntie Mame, pausing at the edge of the circle of light.*)
YOUNG PAT. I thought you were very good, Auntie Mame. Everybody noticed you.
AUNTIE MAME. Oh, my little love. How did you get to New Haven?
YOUNG PAT. Ito brought me up.
AUNTIE MAME. But how could he drive you up when I've already sold the car?
YOUNG PAT. (*Brightly.*) Oh, he didn't drive; we hitch-hiked!
AUNTIE MAME. But Mr. Babcock thinks you're in that horrible school—
YOUNG PAT. (*Patting her shoulder.*) It's all right, Auntie Mame. It's Thanksgiving vacation.
AUNTIE MAME. (*Looking around the stage forlornly.*) Is it? (*He comes to her and puts his arm around her tenderly.*)
YOUNG PAT. Can I be your escort? Can I take you back to your hotel?
AUNTIE MAME. (*Tears in her eyes.*) You can take me all the way back to New York. Oh, Patrick. Are you ashamed of your Auntie Mame?
YOUNG PAT. I'm *proud* of you. Nobody liked the stinky old play at all until you came in. (*Young Pat kisses her lightly on the cheek. Then he takes a step back, bows slightly from the waist, offering his arm.*) Lady Iris? (*She smiles in spite of her dejection, rises, takes his arm.*)

45

AUNTIE MAME. Chahmed, Lord Dudley! (*She makes an Edwardian gesture. They start off together, and she hugs him close as . . .*)

THE LIGHTS FADE

ACT I

SCENE 7

Scene: Telephone switchboard. Buzzing in darkness. We see Auntie Mame wrestling with the plugs. Several are already in place.

AUNTIE MAME. Widdicombe, Gutterman, Applewhite, Bibberman and Black—good morning. One moment, I'll connect you with Mr. Gutterman.(*She plugs.*) Widdicombe, Gutterman, Applewhite, Bibberman and Black, good— Yes, Mr. Bibberman, I'll get you Mr. Applewhite. (*She crosses two plugs, one from each board to the other.*) Widdicombe, Gutterman, Applewhite, Bibberman and Black. Good morning. Long Distance—(*She plugs.*) Mr. Widdicombe, I have your San Francisco call. (*She plugs.*) Yes, Mr. Bibberman. (*Innocently.*) Oh, did I give you Mr. Gutterman instead of Mr. Applewhite? I'm sorry, Mr. Bibbercome—uh, Bibbebib. (*She pulls down a plug from one side, and starts to put it in the other side. But there is already a plug in the hole she wants to put it in. She pulls down the offending plug from the hole with her other hand and holds it up, addressing it as if it were a person.*) Mr. Applewhite, what were you doing in that hole with Mr. Gutterman? (*She now has two plugs, one in each hand. Forgetting where they are supposed to go, she thrusts one plug in her bodice to free her hand for another call. She puts up another plug.*) Mr. Widdicombe, I'll try to reconnect you with San Francisco. Now let me see. . . . (*She starts rearranging the plugs at random, sticking one plug in her mouth.*) Mr. Bibberbip is in there and Mr. Gutterwipe is talking to—. (*The board is going crazy now. She is plugging and unplugging frantically now. Buzz.*)

46

Oh, there you are, Mr. Applewhite. Yes, sir. (*She dials.*) Eldorado 5-2121. Yes, sir. Hold on, Mr. Widdicombe. I'll find San Francisco. (*Buzz.*) Widdicombe, Gutterman, Applewhite. Oh! Supervisor? I did? (*She pushes a key.*) I'm afraid you gave me a wrong number, sir. There is *no* Applewhite 5-, Mr. Eldorado. (*The frantic buzzing continues.*) I don't know what I did with San Francisco. I'll tell you what I *can* do. I can get you Pittsburgh if it's a clear day. (*A particularly insistent buzz. Auntie Mame has managed to knit the plugs together, but extricates one and plugs it in.*) Hello? Oh, hello, Mr. Black. Long time no hear. What? What's that? Tired? No, I'm not tired. Fired? (*A wail.*) Whyyyyy??????

THE LIGHTS FADE

ACT I

SCENE 8

Scene: A roller-skate counter at Macy's. "Silent Night" is playing peacefully against the cacophony of people assailing the roller-skate counter. But there is no clerk behind the counter.

SHOPPER. (*Calling angrily.*) Floor walker! Do I have to wait until New Year's to straighten out these roller-skates? (*Mr. Loomis, a carnation wearing a man, is trying to mollify the customers.*)
LOOMIS. If you'll just be patient, Madam, I'm certain our roller-skate lady will be here momentarily. (*Raising his voice, sing-song to "Silent Night".*) Roller skate lady. Where is the roller-skate lady?
SHOPPER. Your stupid clerk sent me two left roller-skates. Does Macy's think my kid has two left feet—is that what you think?
LOOMIS. Perhaps we'd better take this up with the Complaint Department. If you'll just step this way, Madam. (*The Shopper storms off with Loomis.*) Christmas. God deliver us. (*Auntie*

47

Mame enters with a Woman. Auntie Mame is carrying a Tinker-toy box and a sales-book.)

WOMAN. Clerk, clerk. Am I ever going to get out of here? All I want are these roller skates.

AUNTIE MAME. I don't know how I got over there in Tinker Toys. (*Calling rather plaintively.*) Mr. Loomis? Would you help me with this sales slip, please? (*Auntie Mame opens the sales-book. This is the most bedraggled sales-book in the history of retailing-selling. Carbons, tissues spill out in hectic disarray. Auntie Mame turns back to her customer.*) Oh, Mrs. Jennings, why don't you let me send these to you C.O.D.! Then you won't have to pay any money at all!

WOMAN. Well, I would eventually—

AUNTIE MAME. Don't you worry your head about it, Mrs. Jennings. I'll take care of everything. (*Up.*) Never mind, Mr. Loomis. (*She scribbles a slip.*)

WOMAN. Now just a minute—

AUNTIE MAME. Here's your slip now. See? You don't even have any bundles to carry. (*The Woman goes off.*) Oh, I just love C.O.D. (*During the above, a fine-looking Southern gentleman comes on. This is a hell of a guy; you can tell it from the genuine-ness of his smile. He's rosy-cheeked, with steel-grey hair. His camel's-hair coat and Cavanaugh hat indicate a cosy opulence. This is Beauregard Jackson Pickett Burnside. Auntie Mame turns to him. Reflexively, her eyelids flutter slightly.*)

BEAU. (*In a deep musical Southern drawl.*) Ma'am, would you be good enough to assist me in ordering twenty-four pairs of those fine-looking roller-skates?

AUNTIE MAME. (*Taken aback.*) Twenty four! My, what a proud father you must be!

BEAU. (*Chortles.*) Oh, they're not my children, ma'am; I'm a single gentleman. But a lot of little tykes at the Oglethorpe Or-phange—just outside of Savannah—are gonna pop their eyes out when this package arrives. (*He reaches in his pocket for a roll of bills which would choke a mastadon.*) Now, how much does that come to, little lady? (*Auntie Mame, fumbling with the sales-book, looks at the roll of bills dismayed.*)

AUNTIE MAME. You want to pay? *Cash?*

48

BEAU. Oglethorpe Orphange. R.F.D. 2, Savannah, Georgia. (*Auntie Mame starts to write, then stops and looks round like a trapped animal.*)

AUNTIE MAME. Are you sure you wouldn't rather have these go C.O.D.?

BEAU. (*Laughs heartily.*) Now, what would those little nippers think if their Uncle Beau sent 'em a Christmas present *co*-llect on *de*-livery.

AUNTIE MAME. Mr. Loomis—!

BEAU. (*He is now most gallant.*) If it would be any aid to you, ma'am, I suppose I could *take* the package with me.

AUNTIE MAME. Oh, no. That's worse. (*She looks around as if she were admitting former membership in the Communist Party.*) You see, I haven't worked here very long. And the only kind of sales slip I know how to make out is C.O.D.

BEAU. Well, now. Maybe I can be of some assistance, little lady. I've got a passing familiarity with *fi*-nancial matters. (*He comes behind the counter and takes the sales-book out of her hands and starts to write up the order. This gives Auntie Mame a chance to size up Beau, with some admiration.*)

AUNTIE MAME. You'd better not come back here.

BEAU. First you gotta get your duplicates and triplicates straightened out elsewise Mr. Macy won't have any way of knowin' what you sold.

AUNTIE MAME. That's why they have all that gay tissue-paper!

BEAU. First the name—(*Writes.*) Beauregard Jackson Pickett Burnside.

AUNTIE MAME. That's a long name to get on such a little slip. (*Beau writes with amazing efficiency, and Auntie Mame peeks over his shoulder. Mr. Loomis comes on. He rises to his full five feet five.*)

MR. LOOMIS. Miss Dennis, may I inquire what is going on here?

AUNTIE MAME. (*Floundering.*) Well, Mr. Loomis, this nice gentleman simply offered to—

BEAU. This little lady—Miss Dennis, is that your name?—she was having a mite of trouble making out my sales slip for a couple of dozen roller skates—

MR. LOOMIS. (*Frigidly.*) Was there something *unusual* about the order?

AUNTIE MAME. Yes. He wants to pay *cash*!

MR. LOOMIS. (*Incredulously.*) Am I to understand that a Macy's employee doesn't know how to make a *cash sale*?????

AUNTIE MAME. I'm a whiz at C.O.D.'s. You can see— (*Mr. Loomis seizes the sales-book and leafs through it in amazement.*)

MR. LOOMIS. Miss Dennis, this sales book is a shambles. You are obviously incompetent to dispense merchandise. You will report to personnel immediately for your dismissal.

BEAU. (*Trying to gloss over the matter.*) Now, she was just doin' the best she knew how. . . .

MR. LOOMIS. Well, it's not good enough for the R. H. Macy Company! (*Loomis starts off, still leafing through the sales-book.*) Good heavens, it'll take auditing a week to straighten out this mess. (*Beau follows, protesting.*)

BEAU. Now, you listen here to me, sir. I feel entirely responsible for bringing about this unfortunate misunderstandin'. (*Auntie Mame gets her purse from under the counter and starts off in the opposite direction. Thinking of a moneyless Christmas up ahead, she is sad and dispirited. Suddenly she remembers something and calls across to Beau as he disappears on the tail of Mr. Loomis.*)

AUNTIE MAME. (*Calling.*) Don't forget the roller-skates for those little nippers. (*Sniffs, then belligerently.*) Get 'em at Gimbels!!!!! (*The Shoppers drift off and lighting on the Macy's area fades. Behind the crowd Auntie Mame has slipped on a somewhat threadbare cloth overcoat. We hear a legato disconsolate "Deck The Halls" as a spot follows Mame, down-hearted and desolate.*)

ACT I

SCENE 9

Scene: *The Beekman Place Apartment lights up softly. Some of the furnishings and expensive hangings are gone. There is a Christmas tree. Young Pat is just finishing decorating it. Moving continuously from the previous scene, Auntie Mame walks into the apartment, stands looking at Young Pat and the grubby little tree. Young Pat turns and sees her.*

YOUNG PAT. Auntie Mame! Gee, I didn't expect you home so soon.

AUNTIE MAME. Well, they kinda gave me my Christmas vacation a little bit early. But I'm glad, really. Because now it fits with *your* vacation—and we won't have to miss even a day together.

YOUNG PAT. How do you like the tree? I decorated it myself. Aren't you surprised? (*Auntie Mame sinks down on an ottoman and involuntarily her hand covers her face.*)

AUNTIE MAME. It's beautiful, dear, it's simply beautiful. (*She chokes up. Young Pat, fully aware of her low spirits, determines to cheer her up. He reaches behind the tree for an oblong jeweler's package.*)

YOUNG PAT. I'm going to give you your Christmas present right now. You don't even have to wait till Christmas morning. (*He hands it to her.*) Here. Open it. (*Really speechless, Auntie Mame unwraps the tissue.*)

AUNTIE MAME. Patrick! Where did you get the money?

YOUNG PAT. Mr. Leavitt at the Pawn Shop gave me a very good price for my microscope and my hockey stick.

AUNTIE MAME. Patrick!

YOUNG PAT. I was getting kinda tired of microbes. (*Auntie Mame opens the package and holds up a rhinestone bracelet in excellent taste. She shakes her head, with dazed happiness.*)

AUNTIE MAME. Oh, my.

YOUNG PAT. They're not *quite* diamonds.

AUNTIE MAME. Oh, darling, that's the most beautiful bracelet I've ever owned. (She kisses him.)

YOUNG PAT. Wiggle it! (*She does. No sound.*) See. It doesn't makes any noise. I told the man you had to have a quiet one—for when you go on the stage again. (*She puts it on. He helps her fasten the clasp.*) And when you wear it with your mink coat—why nobody will ever know you work at Macy's!

AUNTIE MAME. I've given up Macy's, dear. And my mink coat

is down at Mr. Leavitt's with your hockey stick. (*Auntie Mame gets up and shakes the depression as if she were discarding a garment. Calling.*) Norah! Ito! If we're going to have Christmas, let's have it all the way around. (*She goes to a drawer and takes out several small boxes. Norah and Ito come on, Ito drawing on his house coat.*)

ITO. Yes, Missy Dennis? (*Auntie Mame hands each of them a package. She hands a suit box to Young Pat.*)

AUNTIE MAME. Merry Christmas, everybody.

NORAH. But it isn't until Tuesday, mum.

ITO. Missy Dennis get mixed up with calendar again. Not Christmas yet.

AUNTIE MAME. Well, we *need* it now—so let's go ahead and have it. (*They start to unwrap their packages eagerly.*) I did want to pay you some of your back salary, but—

NORAH. Now, not another word about it, mum. You know we wouldn't think of leavin' you.

ITO. (*Cheerfully.*) No place else get job anyhow. (*Ito lifts out an inexpensive wrist watch.*) Ohhhhh.

AUNTIE MAME. It isn't seventeen jewels, Ito—but I'm not sure that time is worth all that decoration these days.

ITO. Thank you, Missy. (*Norah opens a box of perfume, cologne and bath salts, unscrews and smells each one.*)

NORAH. It's so French-smellin'! I'll be the most aromatic thing on Beekman Place. (*Young Pat has been wrestling with the suit box. Now he has it open and he holds up a pair of long pants.*)

YOUNG PAT. Golly! Long pants! At last. (*Eagerly.*) Can I try 'em on, Auntie Mame? Right now?

AUNTIE MAME. Right now. (*Young Pat dashes upstairs. Ito and Norah exchange glances, then decide to speak.*)

NORAH. Well, we got a little present for you, too, mum—Ito and me. Now I hope you're not gonna be angry for what we done.

AUNTIE MAME. Just what is it you have done?

NORAH. (*Blurts it out.*) Well, Ito had a bit of money put by— and so did I—for a rainy day, you might say. But we both figgered it couldn't get much wetter than it is right now.

ITO. We pay grocery and butcher bill. (*He hands her a whole sheaf of bills speared on a nail.*) Now Mr. Schultz no give nasty looks with lamb chops. (*Auntie Mame sinks to the ottoman in unbelieving gratitude. She stares at the spiked bills, which look like a ragged miniature Christmas tree.*)

AUNTIE MAME. (*Moved deeply.*) You're both so dear to me. I'll pay you back some day—if I ever can. You know I will. (*Norah comes toward her, gently.*)

NORAH. You're a lovin' woman, mum. You're odd, but you're *lovin'*! And all we wish is you could find a *man.* As wonderful and lovin' and fine a gentleman as you are a fine lady. (*Thinking.*) Whatever happened to that nice Mr. Lindsay Woolsey? He was a dear soul.

AUNTIE MAME. He *was* a dear man, Norah. But I sent him away. I said no so many times when I had money, I couldn't say yes when I went broke. (*At this moment, Young Pat comes down the stairs, bursting with pride in his first long pants. He beams.*)

YOUNG PAT. Look! (*Auntie Mame rises and crosses to the landing, where he stands—almost as tall as she is.*)

AUNTIE MAME. Besides, I have my own fine gentleman, Norah. (*She holds up her wrist.*) Who buys me diamonds. (*Smiling.*) Or "almost" diamonds. (*In apparent high spirits, Auntie Mame moves blithely to the radio and snaps it on.*) What we need now is some music—some Christmas carols! (*The radio squeals a little, as she spins the dial through some spot announcements—finally coming to rest on a chorale version of "Deck the Halls With Boughs of Holly." Auntie Mame starts to sing, and directs the others to join in with her—which they do enthusiastically joining hands and dancing in a circle.*)

ALL. (*Singing.*)
"Deck the halls with boughs of holly,
Fa-la-la-la-la—la-la-la-la
'Tis the season to be jolly,
Fa-la-la-la-la—la-la-la-la."

(*Auntie Mame begins to break up. She turns away from the others, trying to conceal her tears. This ain't no season for her to be jolly. Pat, Norah and Ito rally around trying to comfort her.*)

YOUNG PAT. (*Hugging her.*) Don't cry, Auntie Mame! Please don't cry.

AUNTIE MAME. (*Trying to dry her tears.*) Oh, hell, we don't even have any Kleenex! (*But Norah offers her apron to Auntie Mame, and she uses it to wipe away the tears. The doorbell chimes. Norah scampers towards the kitchen, and Ito starts for the door. Auntie Mame turns to Ito.*) If that's Santa Claus, tell him we've already had it. (*Ito ushers in the rubicund but apologetic figure of Beauregard Burnside. He takes over in a generous and expansive way, hardly giving anyone else an opportunity to speak.*)

BEAU. Ma'am, you don't know how happy I am to see you.

AUNTIE MAME. (*Uncertainly.*) Well, I . . .

BEAU. (*Doffing his wide-brimmed hat.*) Little Lady, do you know I've been skittlin' all over town trying to find you. Do you realize there are ninety-seven Dennises in the Man-hattan Di-rec-tory? And I was beginning to worry you *might* live in that place over there called "Brooklyn."

AUNTIE MAME. But why did you . . .?

BEAU. I came to apologize. I told 'em right out it was all their fault, those Macy folk. A lady with your charm and refinement should have an executive position with a lot of hired help to rassle with all them pesky writin' and figurin' details. (*He starts toward the door.*) Will you excuse me a second, ma'am, while I skittle out and pay that cab driver so he can go home to his family?

AUNTIE MAME. (*Stunned.*) You left a taxi meter running—in the middle of the depression? (*Beau raises his hand in a benediction.*)

BEAU. Ma'am, when you're in oil, a stock market crash is somebody else's noise. (*Auntie Mame is non-plussed.*) And if you wouldn't consider me *pre*-sumptious, I'd be most honored if you'd let me squire you out to dinner tonight.

AUNTIE MAME. No, thank you, we're just having a Christmas celebration, and I can't leave my little family.

BEAU. Ma'am, I like that. I like a woman who has feelin's about family. Why, I've got practically every kind of relative invented. You oughta come down Georgia-way and meet 'em all one day. You'd just love Peckerwood.

AUNTIE MAME. Peckerwood? Who's Peckerwood?

BEAU. Why, that's the name of my little ol' plantation. (*He turns and takes in Pat, Norah, and Ito in an expansive gesture.*) Bring your little family along to dinner, ma'am; the more the merrier! (*Auntie Mame is still spinning from the speed of all this.*)

AUNTIE MAME. But I'm not really dressed. . . .

BEAU. (*At the door.*) You look just fine to me, ma'am. A little powder on your nose, and you're just fine. I'll tell that taxi to wait. (*Beau exits. They all look at each other in excited bewilderment.*)

YOUNG PAT. He's nice—I like him!

AUNTIE MAME. Shh!

NORAH. Marry him, Mum! The minute he asks you!

AUNTIE MAME. Norah, for God's sake!

YOUNG PAT. What's his name, Auntie Mame? You don't even know his name.

AUNTIE MAME. (*Wisely.*) Yes, I do. Family, we are about to break bread with *Beauregard Jackson Pickett Burnside!* (*Norah and Ito laugh delightedly. Swiftly Auntie Mame goes into action.*) Norah, get your coat. Ito, change your jacket. Where's my bag? (*She powders her nose as everyone flies around getting ready to go out.*) Patrick, wear your scarf—it's cold outside. (*Norah comes on in a scrubby cloth coat, carrying a corsage. She hands it to Auntie Mame.*)

NORAH. I was going to give you this wee thing at dinner.

AUNTIE MAME. (*She pulls an ornament off the tree and pins it on Norah's coat.*) Here's one for you, too. (*Young Pat appears in overcoat and muffler, and races for the door.*)

YOUNG PAT. (*Excitedly.*) Come on! We hadn't ought to keep Mr. Burnside waiting! (*Ito returns in a black alpaca coat.*)

ITO. (*Beaming.*) Me never believe in Santa Claus. Me beginning to change mind.

AUNTIE MAME. Well, I never expected Santa Claus to have a southern accent. (*They all tear out the door, Auntie Mame bringing up the rear.*)

ANNOUNCER. (*Through the radio.*) Merry Christmas from Manny, Moe and Jack, your credit clothier!

AUNTIE MAME. (*Magnanimously, in a rich southern accent.*)

55

Merry Christmas to you-all, Manny, Moe and Jack! And a happy little ole New Year! (*She exits after the others, and the Lights fade.*)

ACT I

Scene 10

Scene: There is drippy southern music. We see a picturesque tableau of the white-columned portico of the Burnside Mansion at Peckerwood, with the aristocracy of Oglethorpe County posed gracefully on the lawn awaiting the arrival of Auntie Mame. The stage comes alive with a twittering crowd of Southern belles and Georgia gentlemen, all dressed in Sunday best. It is suggested that this be just a painted drop. In it, stage R, are a curtained door and a Dutch-window, half-open at the top. There is a bench just outside the window.

There is a gathering of the clan to give the o.o. to Uncle Beau's Yankee girlfriend. The tone is roughly the same as that with which General Sherman was received in Atlanta seventy years before.

Prominent in the crowd is Cousin Jefferson Davis Clay Pickett, who booms like the cannons at Fort Sumter.

Cousin Fan, a fussy, insecure poor relative, emerges from L., and twitters ineffectually around the veranda.

COUSIN JEFF. Must be somethin' mighty special about this Dennis woman if'n Beau skittles her all the way down here from New York City. (*Turns to the veranda.*) Mornin', Cousin Fan.
COUSIN FAN. Peculiar mornin', Cousin Jeff. *Mighty* peculiar. Is it generally known that Beau and his lady friend have a *child* with 'em? (*There are gasps, and a general reaction of shocked astonishment.*)
COUSIN JEFF. No-o-o-o!
COUSIN FAN. Don't think it's what you're thinkin'. The boy's thirteen, and Beau's only known her since Christmas. (*There is an air of disappointment at this. Cousin Fan sniffs.*) Besides—she

56

hain't even *met* Mother Burnside yet. (*There is an eager reaction among the clan.*)

COUSIN JEFF. Ho-ho. Seems as if we're all right on time to see the fireworks.

COUSIN FAN. Well, you all know what a delicate *di*-gestive system Mother Burnside has. (*She rolls her eyes upwards. Jeff turns confidentially to his wife.*)

COUSIN JEFF. Ho-ho. When she gets riled, ain't nobody in the State of Georgia—maybe in the whole Confederacy—can outburp Mother Burnside. (*The genteel chit-chat freezes suddenly as Sally Cato MacDougal floats in from L. She carries a parasol. This is a peaches-and-cream Southern belle. Every eye is on her. She is followed by her grubby little brother, Emory, who is about Young Pat's age.*)

SALLY CATO. Well, now—!

COUSIN JEFF. Why, Sally Cato MacDougal!

SALLY CATO. Hello, Jeff honey.

COUSIN FAN. Didn't rightly 'spect *you* to be comin' round for the doin's.

SALLY. (*Dripping sweetness.*) Why, however could I manage to stay away; when our own dear Beau is bringin' his little Yankee friend back down here to Peckerwood? Why, I wouldn't feel like a true daughter of the South if I didn't ooze out all the hospitality that's just simmerin' in my inners!

COUSIN JEFF. You're a big-hearted woman, Sally Cato.

SALLY. (*Fluttery.*) Well, now, jus' because Beauregard and me been engaged since grammar school, don't mean I refrain from wishin' him and his new found friend every happiness. (*Young Pat comes running on from R. He is slightly Lord Fauntleroyed. He stops short when he sees the crowd of people.*)

YOUNG PAT. My Auntie Mame—Miss Dennis, I mean—she says she'll be here in just a minute. (*Sally Cato smiles lovingly at Young Pat.*)

SALLY. Well now—what a lovable, genteel little gentleman. (*She calls to her brother gutterly.*) Emory, come on over here. (*Back to Pat.*) You and my little brother are gonna get along like a pair of colts in a pasture. I can just tell. (*She hits Emory with her*

57

parasol. Then flutters among the guests. Emory sullenly faces Young Pat.)

EMORY. What's your name, Yankee boy?

YOUNG PAT. Patrick Dennis.

EMORY. If ya gimme a dime, I'll take you down to my shanty and show ya my dirty pitchas.

YOUNG PAT. Maybe I'd better not—right now. (*Making conversation.*) Your sister's nice.

EMORY. (*Incredulous.*) *Nice?!* You're plumb crazy. They teach ya to spell up there, Yankee boy?

YOUNG PAT. Sure.

EMORY. (*Lowering his voice.*) My sister is a B-I-T-C-H. (*There is a clatter and rumble from within the portals of Peckerwood. Mother Burnside's gravelly baritone is raised in acid invective.*)

MOTHER BURNSIDE'S VOICE. (*Off from* L.). Where's my soda tablets? What son of a no-good-hound-dog stole my soda tablets?

BEAU'S VOICE. (*Also from off* L.) They're right in your lap, Mother. (*All turn toward* L. *Beau pushes a wheelchair onto the verandah; in the wheelchair sits Mother Burnside, a beady-eyed imperious woman built along the lines of a General Electric refrigerator. Dressed all in black, she looks like a cross between Caligula and a cockatoo. Everybody proffers a tentative greeting.*)

MOTHER BURNSIDE. Beauregard, when you gonna trot out that New York filly? (*Her beady eyes scan the assemblage contemptuously.*) All I can see around here is *family.*

ALL. Mornin', Mother Burnside.

MOTHER BURNSIDE. (*Suddenly brightens.*) 'Ceptin' you, Sally Cato. Still paintin' your finger-nails?

SALLY. You're lookin' cute as a bug, Miz Burnside. (*Mother Burnside burps.*) Well, welcome home, Beau-darlin'!

BEAU (*Uncomfortably.*) Hello there, Sally Cato.

MOTHER BURNSIDE. (*To Beau, wagging her head.*) When we got peaches right here, ripe for the pickin', I can't see why any man would go hankerin' after some *Northern* alligator pear. (*She clasp a hand to her stomach, as if a gastritic eruption were about to take place.*)

BEAU. (*Worried.*) Now, now, Mama—let's keep our hominy grits goin' the right way! (*He calls off* R.) Mame? Mame honey, we're all out here, waitin' for you.

AUNTIE MAME'S VOICE. (*From off* R. *Calls, southern as a candied yam.*) Ah'm comin', Beau-sugah. Ah'm just bustin' to meet yoah sweet little ole mothah! (*Mame swirls on from* R., *wearing a hoopskirt and looking very much like Scarlett O'Hara. She stops, with a little faked gasp.*)

BEAU. Mother, may I present Miss Mame Dennis? (*Auntie Mame falters only for a fraction of a second, then advances and takes Mother Burnside's leathery hand.*)

AUNTIE MAME. I don't mind sayin, Miz Burnside, you're everything I ever expected and quite a bit more. (*Mother Burnside burps.*)

BEAU. (*Waving across the lawn.*) And these are all my kinfolk. That's my cousin, Jefferson Davis Clay Pickett, his wife; Cousin Fan; Aunt Euphemia; Uncle Moultrie; Lizzie Beaufort—you'll get to know 'em all. You'll all be first-namin' each other soon as we pour another gallon o' bourbon into the punch bowl! (*Beau exits* L.)

AUNTIE MAME. I cain't tell you how chowmin' it is to meet all of you-all! (*This doesn't sound quite right to her, but she carries it off nicely. Sally swoops up, taking Mame's hands with a gush of affection.*)

SALLY. And I'm Sally Cato MacDougal. I could just tell from the first *instant* I set eyes on you that we was gonna be the *closest* of bosom friends, Mame. May I call you Mame?

AUNTIE MAME. Please do.

SALLY. You call me "Sally Cato," heah?—All my most intimate friends *do*. (*Several glances are exchanged. Auntie Mame is completely taken in.*)

AUNTIE MAME. Why, that's awfully kind of you, Sally Cato.

SALLY. Was it *horses* brought you and Beauregard together?

AUNTIE MAME. (*Blankly.*) Horses?

SALLY. Well, I can't imagine Beau even *lookin'* at a lady who wasn't practically *bawn* on a horse.

AUNTIE MAME. (*Laying it on.*) Oh, I just love riding. Up in New York hardly a day goes by that I don't have the sadd—the *boots* on. Up every morning at the crack of dawn for a brisk canter through Central Park.

SALLY. Well, now—that settles it. Here I've been wrackin' my poor brain tryin' to figure what *special* I could do to let you know how I feel about your bein' down here. And what could be better than a *hunt*!

AUNTIE MAME. (*Paling a little.*) A hunt???

SALLY. (*Raising her voice.*) Listen, evabodeh! Beauregard's gone and *surprised* us all. It seems Miz Dennis here is a prominent North'n horsewoman.

AUNTIE MAME. (*Trying to put the brakes on this.*) Well, I wouldn't say *prominent*—No—I'm not prominent.

SALLY. (*Barreling on.*) So natcherly, we'll have to have a hunt! Dawn, tomorrow morning! And evabody's invited! (*She turns brightly to Auntie Mame.*) Won't we have the lark, all of us—at sunup—leapin' over those hedges, jumpin' over those river gaps, the hounds yappin' around those boulders—(*Auntie Mame steadies herself against one of the columns.*) I tell you, Mame, every eye in this county is going to be on you tomorrow mornin'!

AUNTIE MAME. (*Thinking fast.*) If I'd only *known*. You see, I didn't bring down any of my ridin' togs.

SALLY. Don't you worry, Mame child. I've got *dozens* of things you could wear. What's your shoe size? (*Mame tries to draw her feet under her skirt.*)

AUNTIE MAME. (*Lying.*) Three-B.

SALLY. Marvelous. Same as I wear. I can even fit you out with boots.

AUNTIE MAME. (*Weakly.*) I don't know if Beau would want me to—

SALLY. (*Barreling on.*) You *do* ride astride, Mame dear?

AUNTIE MAME. (*A hopeful gleam in her eyes.*) No—No. Side saddle—always. Daddy, the Colonel, insisted that I learn it. He said it was the only way for a true lady to ride. So graceful. Silly of him, of course, because *nobody* rides side-saddle these days, but it's the only way I know how. (*She sighs, pleased with herself.*)

SALLY. (*Purring.*) Now, isn't that grand! I just happen to have a little old side-saddle that'll do you *fine*. (*Beau comes out from* L., *carrying a trayful of punch glasses. Graciously he passes them around to the guests.*)

BEAU. Refreshment, ladies? (*Mame drinks a whole punch-cup at one gulp.*)

SALLY. Beau darlin', we're havin' ourselves a hunt! At dawn tomorrow! And you want to hear somethin' fantastic? Your sweet little Yankee girl is gonna ride side-saddle.

BEAU. I won't allow it! It's too dangerous.

SALLY. But, darling, she's insisted.

BEAU. Well, anything Mame says she can do, she can do. I tell you—this is an amazing woman. (*Mame quickly downs a second drink.*)

SALLY. Oh, Mame sugah—I'm just going to *hold my breath* until dawn tomorrow.

AUNTIE MAME. Do that, honey.

THE LIGHTS FADE

ACT I

SCENE 11

The lighting makes a transition. It is not quite dawn. In the distance a grumpy rooster crows. The set has not been changed.

A spotlight picks up the area of the Dutch-window and the door at R. Behind the Dutch-window, Mame is dressing, with the aid of a couple of unseen dressers on their knees. Young Pat is seated at the bench just outside the window. Auntie Mame keeps poking her head out of the window to talk to Young Pat, as she is dressing. Young Pat has a book in his hand.

AUNTIE MAME. Stop looking at the pictures and read it to me, darling. I'm listening. (*Young Pat turns to the opening page.*)

YOUNG PAT. "How to Ride A Horse." (*She is struggling to get into a pair of borrowed riding boots. Young Pat begins to read.*) It says you should always get on a horse from the left side.

AUNTIE MAME. *Your* left side or the *horse's* left side?

YOUNG PAT. It doesn't say. Listen to this. (*He reads.*) "When-

61

ever a rider approaches a strange mount"—I guess that means the horse—"he should fix the animal in the eye with a masterful gaze. For a horse can detect the slightest indication of trepidation." (*He breaks off.*) What's "trepidation?"

AUNTIE MAME. That's what your Auntie Mame's got a bad case of right now. Go on, dear, go on.

YOUNG PAT. "The horse is extremely sensitive . . ."

AUNTIE MAME. Where??????????

YOUNG PAT. There are some peachy pictures in this book about how to jump over fences. It says you should *lean.*

AUNTIE MAME. If anybody does any leaning, it's gotta be the horse. (*Auntie Mame tries vainly to pull on one of the boots. After a painful groan, she stops, closes her eyes and mutters something inarticulately under her breath.*)

YOUNG PAT. What did you say, Auntie Mame?

AUNTIE MAME. I'm not talking to you, my little love. I'm talking to God. (*She emerges in riding skirt and the flapping boots only half on. She can hardly walk.*) I think Sally Cato left a foot in this one.

YOUNG PAT. (*Rising.*) I'll help you. (*Auntie Mame sits on the bench and Pat tries to shove the boot on.*)

AUNTIE MAME. So this is what they call "dying with your boots on."

YOUNG PAT. (*Sympathetically*). Why are you going through all this, Auntie Mame?

AUNTIE MAME. Darling, if I can only snag you an Uncle Beau, all our problems will be solved. (*She makes a wistful half-smile.*) Besides, there's one other extremely minor, relatively unimportant little old thing: I happen to be in love with him. (*Pat laughs happily.*)

PAT. Has he asked you anything yet?

AUNTIE MAME. (*Shaking her head.*) No. But he wouldn't have brought us down here—if he didn't intend to.

BEAU. (*From off* L.) Are you dressed yet, Mame, honey? (*Pat quickly hides the book behind his back.*)

AUNTIE MAME. Oh, yes, Beau, darlin'. (*He enters* L., *resplendent in a red riding habit. He has several cameras draped about his neck.*) Oh my, how handsome you look.

BEAU. (*Focusing Camera.*) Likewise, Mame. Hold it! (*Auntie Mame strikes a fancy pose. He snaps a picture.*) You are now immortalized in cell-you-loid. (*He turns to Young Pat.*) Would you excuse us for a second, young fella? There's something I want to talk to your Auntie Mame about.

YOUNG PAT. (*Obligingly.*) Oh, sure. (*He scoots out R.*)

BEAU. (*Taking a deep breath.*) Mame, what I've got to say, I've got to say fast, a-fore that huntin' horn blows. And talkin' fast is somethin' that don't come easy to a south'n gentleman.

AUNTIE MAME. Then talk slow, Beau darlin'—I can listen fast. (*Beau takes her hand.*)

BEAU. I consider myself a very lucky man. It was luck that made me smell oil when I was walkin' across that soy-bean patch Cousin Marvin left me. And it was just pure dumb Georgia luck that roller-skated us together last Christmas.

AUNTIE MAME. (*Hanging on every word.*) I feel that same way, Beau, dear. Go on.

BEAU. Mame, honey . . . what I want to ask you is—(*He is beginning to get red-faced.*) Would you . . . Could you . . .? That is, might you . . . (*She turns away coyly. The hunting horn sounds blatantly off. Beau reacts like a fireman who has heard the bell. He drops Mame's hand abruptly.*) To the hounds! (*He bolts off L. eagerly. Mame is left alone.*)

AUNTIE MAME. Hounds! Sons-of-bitches. (*Her shoulders sag as the lights fade. Mame exits in the momentary darkness. The lighting makes the full transition to rosy dawn. The scene is still Peckerwood, but bathed in a lovely early morning glow.*)

ACT I

SCENE 12

The red-coated huntsman comes on L. and blows another blast on the hunting horn.

Beau and Cousin Jeff come on L., ready for the hunt.

BEAU. (*Taking a deep breath of morning air.*) Can't wait to get on the trail of that fox. We *got* a fox, ain't we, Jeff?

JEFF. Had to use that spare one we was keepin' in the cellar of the ice-house. He's a mite moth-eaten, but he'll do. (*Sally Cato comes on L., assured in her riding habit. She crosses R. to Beau and fiddles with his ascot.*)

SALLY. Beau darlin'—now ain't you just the *handsomest* little old thing.

BEAU. (*Embarrassed.*) Aw-w-w, Sally Cato. (*Turns, searching.*) Hope we got Mame a nice piece of horse-flesh.

SALLY. (*Patting Beau's lapel cosily.*) Don't you worry one minute 'bout your sweet little ole Northern gal. I puhsonally picked her mount. I've seen to it that she's gonna be took care of just fine. (*She smiles at him with every tooth in her head.*)

BEAU. You're a big-hearted woman, Sally Cato. (*There is a gentle whinny from off R. Beau crosses R., calling to the grooms.*) Hold her steady, boy! (*Reaches in his pocket.*) I got a lump of sugah for you, Brown Beauty old girl! (*He goes off, and we hear him mounting—the creak of leather and pawing in the gravel.*) Hup—hup. Atta girl! (*Sally Cato slaps her whip on the ground and laughs. Auntie Mame comes out of the house from R., followed by Young Pat. She's putting up a brave front, and he is still reading from the book, instructing her. She actually manages to smile at Sally Cato as she tries to fake the walk and stance of an experienced horsewoman.*)

AUNTIE MAME. Mornin', Sally Cato.

SALLY. (*Sweetly.*) Mornin', Mame dear. How unusual you look. (*Calls off R.*) You can bring up Miss Dennis' horse now, boys. (*Back to Mame.*) He's the most special thing in mah stable; evahbody talks about him. What an exhilaratin' day we're gonna have. (*She starts off toward the mounting block offstage. The hounds and the Hunters have all crossed over, too.*)

AUNTIE MAME. Just a minute, Sally Cato—Wouldn't my horse like it if I called him by his name? What's his name?

SALLY. (*Smiling.*) Lightnin' Rod. (*Sally Cato goes off R. Auntie Mame looks struck.*)

GIRL. (*Who has entered from* L.) Mawnin', Miss Dennis. (*She skips.*)

AUNTIE MAME. Mawnin'! Mawnin'! (*Auntie Mame imitates the girl's skip.*)

YOUNG PAT. (*Concerned.*) Auntie Mame—could you maybe—sprain your ankle—quick?

AUNTIE MAME. (*Grimly.*) I've got to go through with it. I can't be a disgrace to Beau in front of all his people. (*There is a fierce whinnying off, and wild stomping. Two Grooms back onto the stage from* R. *in panic; One has his upstage hand hidden in his coat. There is a babble of voices on-stage and off.*)

VOICES. Ho! Rein him up. Stand clear of that horse, boy. Steady, steady! (*Auntie Mame stares off, horrified.*)

AUNTIE MAME. (*Dry-throated.*) That—that—that horse's name isn't—Lightnin' Rod?

GROOM. (*Nods, portentously.*) Lightnin' Rod. (*Again, the off-stage horse thunders a whinny and paws the gravel.*)

AUNTIE MAME. (*Swallows.*) Maybe if I gave him a lump of sugar, it would—(*The Groom lifts up his bandaged hand.*)

GROOM. I wouldn't try it if I was you, Ma'am. (*Mame kisses Pat goodbye, then edges* L. *toward the offstage animal, trying to stare it down.*)

AUNTIE MAME. (*Muttering to herself.*) "Fix the animal in the eye with a masterful gaze—" (*She goes off like Sidney Carton en route to the guillotine. There is more pawing and whinnying, accompanied by shouts and grunts, as she presumably manages to get aboard the horse. Young Pat watches with horrified fascination. Cousin Fan helps on the bloodthirsty figure of Mother Burnside from* L., *who has a pair of field glasses. She sits in a rocker.*)

MOTHER BURNSIDE. (*Looking down toward where the horse is stomping.*) Naow that is what I call a spirited animule! (*Auntie Mame off, lets out a fading scream, as the horse hoofs gallop away. Mother Burnside waves a dirty old lace handkerchief, delightedly.*) Goodbye, Yankee Girl! (*The Huntsman's horn sounds off, and the hunt is evidently in progress. Mother Burnside glues the field glasses to her eyes. She rocks delightedly through the following. Emory dashes on from* R. *Young Pat watches tip-toe.*)

65

Emory rushes up to him and grabs his arm.) Hey, Yankee Boy! I seen 'em side-saddlin' up Lightnin' Rod. Your aunt ain't plannin' to ride him, is she?

YOUNG PAT. Plannin'? Look!

EMORY. Kee-ripes. Look at 'em go.

YOUNG PAT. Auntie Mame! Fall off! Fall off! (*The sound of progressing hunt comes from three staggered speakers on the balcony rail. We hear stereophonically the yapping of the dogs and the pounding of horses' hooves and the occasional bleat of the Huntsman's horn. Mother Burnside's field-glasses follow the action and she rocks vigorously and chortles with grisly good humor, punctuated by burps.*)

MOTHER BURNSIDE. Cleared the first hedge-row and not a broken leg yit! Look at 'em go! What's she comin' back this way for? That fool Yankee girl's got 'em goin' in circles. (*Young Pat, Emory, Cousin Fan, Mother Burnside and two of the Grooms are watching in fascinated horror.*) Get out of my flower-garden. Keep them damn horses out of my bougainvilla. Look out fer that yar flood wall.

YOUNG PAT. Lean, Auntie Mame—lean! (*Cousin Fan and Young Pat cover their eyes—then peek out, fearing the worst.*)

MOTHER BURNSIDE. Gol dang if that Yankee gal didn't sail right over it! NO HANDS!

GROOM. She's passin' everybody!

MOTHER BURNSIDE. She's passin' the Mastuh of the Hounds! (*She puts down the glasses angrily.*) Mighty bad form, passin' the Mastuh! (*The glasses go up again, and sweep along, following the action.*)

YOUNG PAT. She's passin' the dogs!

MOTHER BURNSIDE. (*Astounded.*) Mother of Jefferson Davis, she's passin' the Fox! (*Mother Burnside rocks as if she herself were in the saddle. Off, we hear the wheezing of a Model-A Ford approaching at top speed, honking, and screeching of brakes. There is a car-door slam off, and the Vet rushes on from L. He has a gun in a holster, and his face is livid with rage.*)

VET. (*Roaring accusation.*) Miz Burnside! Is that hawse out thar Lightnin' Rod???

MOTHER BURNSIDE. (*Delighted.*) Suah looks like it. (*To the*

Vet.) But we won't need a hawse doctah around here today. We're gonna need the othah kind!

VET. (*Thundering.*) Plain premediated *murdah*, that's what it is! (*He points toward the progressing fox-hunt, which has apparently zig-zagged several times across the field of vision from the portico. Suddenly Mother Burnside stops rocking and leans forward. Now all the Watchers freeze, staring dead-front in horror. The sound of hoofs, hounds and cries grows louder, as if the hunting party were advancing straight upon them.*)

MOTHER BURNSIDE. (*Shrieks.*) That damn Yankee-girl is leadin' 'em straight into the livin' room! (*But it is a near miss. All eyes swing toward off-stage the opposite side from which the hunt departed, but the same side on which the Vet's car is parked. The noise of the approaching hunt grows louder still. Young Pat covers his eyes. Cousin Fan shrieks. Mother Burnside braces one leg against the railing.*)

VET. (*Screaming, his arm raised.*) Watch out—my flivvah's parked in back of them begonia bushes! That's caounty property! That's—

GROOM. Rein her in! (*There's a mighty crash of hoofs against glass and tin; there is the outraged "Ah-oo-gah" of an old Ford horn, which subsides into a dying gasp.*)

YOUNG PAT. (*Cries out.*) Auntie Mame!!!!! (*Almost as if hurtled onto the stage, Auntie Mame staggers forward from L. She is windblown and disheveled. In one hand she has a broken steering wheel from the Vet's car. She is holding something in her other hand, but it is hidden behind the folds of her skirt.*)

MOTHER BURNSIDE. What happened to the fox?

AUNTIE MAME. (*Holding aloft the limp furpiece that was once a fox.*) Trampled to death! (*The Others from the hunt begin to pour on, babbling with astonishment, congratulating the dazed Auntie Mame. Beau rushes up to her.*)

BEAU. Are you all right, Mame-honey????? When I saw that crazy hawse crash into that car, and you flyin' through the air— (*Auntie Mame lamely holds up the steering wheel.*)

AUNTIE MAME. If I hadn't grabbed hold of this, I'd be in North Carolina! (*Sally Cato comes on uncertainly. But everybody is gathered around Auntie Mame admiringly.*)

JEFF. Soo-*pub* hawse-woman! Pufeckly soo-*pub!*

VET. (*Turning on Sally Cato.*) Sally Cato MacDougal, as County veterinarian, Ah *commanded* you two years ago to have that crazy Lightnin' Rod destroyed. Why, she oughta have her name read outta every huntin' pack in the who' county.

BEAU. (*Turning his back on Sally Cato and swelling with pride close to Auntie Mame.*) Everybody—ah want you to meet my little *YANKEE VALKYRIE!* (*They embrace. The Vet shakes his fist at Sally Cato. Auntie Mame is blushing prettily at the flood of compliments.*)

JEFF. What a seat that woman has! What a magnificent *seat!* (*Auntie Mame glances back with a startled take. Then she touches the back of her skirt to see if it's torn there.*)

BEAU. (*Stretching out his arms.*) Listen, evahbodeh! I have an important announcement to make to you-all! This magnificent Diana-of-the-Chase is gonna become Mrs. Beauregard Jackson Pickett Burnside! (*Auntie Mame tosses the fox to Sally like a bridal bouquet.*)

SALLY. Emory, come on home!

EMORY. (*Happily.*) Hot damn! Mah sistah's gonna bust a gut! (*He skeedaddles off, L. following his Sister.*)

MOTHER BURNSIDE. Well, what are you-all standin' around for??? Skittle yo' selves into the house and we'll all have a *glass* o' whiskey! Come on. (*Cousin Fan helps Mother Burnside off L. All congratulate the beaming Beau and the beat-up but victorious Auntie Mame as they file into the house. Nobody's paying much attention to Young Pat, and he hangs back unnoticed. All the guests have gone inside now. Beau takes Auntie Mame's hand.*)

BEAU. Ah'll make you happy, Mame-honey. For a honeymoon, we'll take a year off and go clean around the world! Just you and me. (*He embraces her. Young Pat, hearing this, slips farther downstage, feeling very much alone. Auntie Mame starts to go in the house with Beau but suddenly she glances back and sees Young Pat.*)

AUNTIE MAME. You go in the house, darlin'. I'll be there in just a minute. (*Crossing quickly to him, sympathetically.*) Patrick, my little love—

YOUNG PAT. (*Softly.*) Congratulations, Auntie Mame. (*She*

takes Young Pat's hand and leads him to the bench at R. *She sits, holding him, though he hangs back a bit.*)

AUNTIE MAME. Your Auntie Mame's in love—and very, very happy.

YOUNG PAT. I won't see you for a long time.

AUNTIE MAME. But, darling, you'll be busy at school. And I'll write you every day. I promise. And I'll be back with you before you even know it. Now come on in the house and we'll have some breakfast. And let me see you smile. I haven't gone yet. Up! Up! That's my boy. (*Pat manages a small smile and starts to go. He stops and turns to Auntie Mame who is on her way inside.*)

YOUNG PAT. Can I ask you just one question? (*She nods.*) How did you stay on that horse?

AUNTIE MAME. It was just like the bracelet in New Haven: I got stuck. (*She reaches behind her, confidentially.*) But at the other end! (*They laugh warmly, and Auntie Mame gives Patrick a big hug and they go* L. *into the house together.*)

CURTAIN

End of Act I

ACT II

Scene 1

In the darkness we hear an uncertain blend of ex-boy-sopranos singing the "Saint Boniface Fight Song":
BOYS' VOICES. (*Unseen, singing.*)
> "Fight, fight, fight for Saint Boniface, Boniface!
> We will win for Saint Boniface, Boniface!
> Carry the ball over the line!
> Show 'em what we can do!
> Fight, fight, fight for Saint Boniface Blue!"

As the music fades, the lights come up on:
SCENE: *A study room at Saint Boniface Academy,* R. *Young Pat is seated at a study table wearing a beanie. He looks taller and older, but this is the same lad who gave Auntie Mame's life a purpose and direction in Act One. But somehow the ingenuous charm of childhood seems to have worn off a bit. There is a trace of cockiness and conceit about Young Pat now, and occasionally he shows a faint resemblance to a Mr. Babcock who has been shrunk in the laundry. Young Pat is checking over a letter he has written.*

YOUNG PAT. (*Reading.*) "To Mrs. Mame Burnside, American Express, Cairo. Dear Auntie Mame. It's wonderful to get your letters every day. Thank you for the chop-sticks you sent from Yokohama. They sure come in handy. I guess you and Uncle Beau are enjoying the world all right—and vice versa." (*He makes an insertion in long hand.*) Ha, ha—joke. (*He continues reading.*) "Mr. Babcock says if I work hard here at Saint Boniface he will enroll me at Rumson University, which is Mr. Babcock's alma mater. He says I'll be very lucky if I'm admitted—considering everything." (*He turns over the page to read the other side.*) "I plan to spend the holidays again with the Babcocks in Darien.

70

Junior Babcock and I have swell times there, and I have met the kids from practically all the best families in Connecticut. (*As the lights fade, we hear a haunting muezzin cry, and the right half of the traveler closes in front of Young Pat's study room.*)

ACT II

Scene 2

The action is continuous, as the spot hits stage L. revealing:
Scene: *The Pyramids. This is an inset, with levels, suggesting the slope of the great Pyramid.*
We find Uncle Beau in a pith helmet and wearing a garland of Leicas and light meters. He has climbed above Auntie Mame to shoot down at her as she studies Young Pat's letter. She is garbed in a fetching camel driver's outfit from Russek's, and scowls slightly as she reads aloud.

AUNTIE MAME. (*Reading.*) "Junior Babcock and I have swell times there, and I have met the kids from practically all the best families in Connecticut." (*She calls up to Beau.*) Oh dear, Beau —I have a feeling we should be getting back.
UNCLE BEAU. (*Fiddling with his camera.*) Just one more shot.
AUNTIE MAME. Home, I mean. I feel Patrick needs me.
UNCLE BEAU. Move a little to the right, Mame darlin'. I'm gettin' too much Pyramid and not enough you.
AUNTIE MAME. Beau. I do wish you'd stop climbing up on things. It makes me so nervous.
UNCLE BEAU. Remember the higher you go, the more interesting the shot. Now, look natural. (*Auntie Mame strikes a Vogue-cover pose, and puts on a frozen smile.*) Oh, that's just fine. (*He clicks the picture, fussing inexpertly with the camera.*) You know, Mame, I think that's gonna turn out even better than the one of you standing by the ole Moulmein Pagoda, looking eastward to the sea.
AUNTIE MAME. Now you come down from there. (*As he does,*

71

she takes his arm affectionately.) Little did I think when I married you, that I was getting such a wonderful photographer, too. (*Lightly.*) Oh, did you remember to put film in the camera this time?

UNCLE BEAU. I sure did! (*He opens the camera to make sure, and the entire roll of exposed film unreels itself in the bright Egyptian sunlight.*) Dang! (*The lights fade on the Pyramid area, L. In the momentary darkness we hear the strains of the Rumson University alma mater.*)

ACT II

Scene 3

GLEE CLUB. (*Singing from off.*)
      "O Rumson U, dear Rumson U,
      To thee we'll e'er be staunch and true.
      E'en when our college days are through,
      We'll still remember you, Rumson U."
The lights come up on the area right.

SCENE: *A dormitory room at Rumson University. The action is continuous.*

Several years have passed, and for the first time we see Patrick Dennis, the young man. He lounges casually at a typewriter, with text books littering the desk in front of him. However, he is engaged in the happy pastime of writing another letter to his Auntie Mame. He wears a beanie blazoned with the Rumson "R." He has matured into a remarkably handsome, intelligent and personable young man. There's only one trouble: he knows it. Pulling the letter from the typewriter, Patrick reads.

PATRICK. (*Reading.*) "To Mrs. Beauregard Jackson Pickett Burnside, care of American Express, Zurich, Switzerland. Dear Auntie Mame. I think it's great that you and Uncle Beau are getting ar eighth honeymoon on your eighth anniversary. Everybody here was certainly impressed with the statue of the laughing

Buddha you sent me from Siam: It was a bit large, however, to get through the door of the dorm. If you decide to go on that caravan to Baghoad, don't let them give you a camel named 'Lightnin' Rod'. Rumson U. is not as dull and denominational as you thought. Miss Pritchard's finishing school is nearby and it's overflowing with the prettiest debutantes you ever saw. Since you came and spent my last vacation with me, I have grown several more inches, my voice has changed several more times—and you may not recognize what my glands have done to me. (*He turns the page over.*) Give Uncle Beau a kiss for me; I'm sure he will enjoy it more coming from you since I've been shaving almost daily now and my beard tickles. (*A thought occurs to him and pencils an insert into the letter.*) . . . or so the debs tell me. (*He chuckles at his own joke, then continues reading.*) Say 'Hi' to the Matterhorn for me. Your loving nephew, Patrick." (*The lights fade. From off, we hear some hyperbolic yodeling.*)

ACT II

Scene 4

Scene: *The Matterhorn. The levels which represented the Pyramids have been redressed and masked to depict an Alpine glacier.*

Uncle Beau is actually out of sight amid the peaks high above Auntie Mame, who is decked out in stunning fur parka, and reads Patrick's letter. Again, the action is nearly continuous.

AUNTIE MAME. (*Reading.*) Glands . . . Debutantes! (*She calls up to Uncle Beau who is out of sight above.*) Beau, I have a feeling that Patrick's right on the brink of something.
UNCLE BEAU (*Offstage.*) Just a little higher and I think this is gonna be the best shot yet! Mame honey, do you mind stepping back a bit? (*Auntie Mame looks over her shoulder and down behind her. From the expression on her face, we know it is a sheer drop of half-a-mile straight down. She calls up to Beau, sweetly.*)

AUNTIE MAME. I'd rather not.

UNCLE BEAU. Don't you never mind—I'll skittle up a might.

AUNTIE MAME. Please, Beau, no higher.

UNCLE BEAU. Remember, honey, the high shots are the best. (*Auntie Mame starts to protest, but we see an ice-axe being lowered from above.*) Take this, honey. Pesky thing keeps gettin' in my way.

AUNTIE MAME. (*Taking it, gingerly.*) No! Hang on to the other end, dear, for your balance.

UNCLE BEAU. (*Offstage. Calling down.*) Don't you worry, Mame—I'm as sure-footed as a mountain goat. Hold it— just like that! Steady—wait'll I re-focus. (*Again Mame strikes a pose, while Beau yodels blithely. But suddenly the yodel resolves into a thin, fading scream, which reverberates down the glacier.*)

AUNTIE MAME. (*Tentatively.*) Beau???? (*The other end of the rope drops with limp significance. Auntie Mame looks up, horrified.*) Beau!!!!! (*The lights fade quickly. Melancholy voices from backstage hum "Massa's In The Cold, Cold Ground," with a wistful yodel in counterpoint.*)

ACT II

SCENE 5

SCENE: *The Beekman Place apartment.*

There are dust covers over some of the chairs. Lindsay, who is graying nicely into a sort of Manhattan Ronald Colman, adjusts a dictaphone. Vera, who is now somewhere between forty and death, has not aged at all—due to the diurnal ministrations of Charles of the Ritz.

VERA. (*Looking at Lindsay skeptically.*) What's that thing supposed to be, Lindsay?

LINDSAY. A dictaphone.

VERA. She'll never use it. You've lugged all this junk in here for nothing.

LINDSAY. Vera, she can't go on living in a vacuum. Mame's always got to have a project!

VERA. She's got a project. Now she's the tragic queen, and she's having such fun being miserable. All she's done for two years is wander around Europe re-visiting the places she's been with Beau. Eight times she climbed that lousy Matterhorn—to toss rose petals down the glacier.

LINDSAY. Well, she must have loved him. (*Vera starts to take off some of the dust-covers.*)

VERA. Let's get some more of these dust-covers off—the place looks like a morgue. (*Lindsay helps her.*)

LINDSAY. You know, Vera, I'm a coward—I should've gone to the boat to meet her. (*Vera is prowling for a drink. The door buzzer rings. Lindsay crosses to open the door for Agnes Gooch, a dowdy owl-eyed secretary who slouches in the foyer, with a shorthand pad under her arm.*)

VERA. (*At bar.*) I haven't seen her since I dragged myself over for the funeral. Wasn't it just like Mame to keep him till I got there? (*Looking at the label of the lone bottle.*) Southern Comfort. Oh, well.

LINDSAY. (*At the door, to Gooch.*) Oh, yes—come in.

VERA. (*Turning from the bar, expectantly.*) Mame!? (*Gooch schlumps into the apartment. Vera's jaw drops.*) My God, she can't have changed *that* much!

GOOCH. (*In a flat, nasal drone.*) I'm from Speed-o.

VERA. (*Blankly.*) What?

LINDSAY. I called this secretarial service. I want to show Mame we really mean business, let her know I'm really serious about this thing. (*Turning to Agnes.*) Your name is . . . ?

GOOCH. Agnes Gooch.

LINDSAY. Now, Miss Gooch, you'll be taking dictation from Mrs. Burnside—and she's a pretty fast talker.

GOOCH. Oh, Speed-o won't let anybody out who can't do at least 100 words a minute. (*She lowers her eyes modestly.*) I'm over 200.

VERA. You're not! Well, if Mame does any dictating—which I doubt—it'll be sprinkled with French, Egyptian, Japanese and four-letter words.

75

GOOCH. (*After a moment's thought.*) I'm afraid I'm not your girl. (*Gooch starts to leave, but Lindsay moves to stop her.*)

LINDSAY. Please stay, Miss Gooch. This should be an interesting experience for you. Mrs. Burnside will pour out a flood of words and ideas, and you must soak them all up. You'll be her . . . (*He gropes for the word.*) Her *sponge!* (*Gooch looks at Lindsay askance. Vera throws up her hands.*)

VERA. Oh, Lindsay, how can Mame write a book? She can't even sit still long enough to write a post-card.

LINDSAY. (*Leading Gooch toward the desk.*) I've got somebody to help her. (*He glances at his watch.*) Oh, good Lord, I told the fellow to be here at three o'clock.

VERA. (*Interested.*) What fellow?

LINDSAY. Miss Gooch, you're on salary as of right now. (*Auntie Mame and Patrick appear in the foyer. She is in black, heavily veiled, and Patrick wears his Ivy League best. They have been chatting warmly. Patrick presses the buzzer three times.*)

AUNTIE MAME. Why are you ringing, Patrick? Don't you have a key?

PATRICK. Of course. I forgot. (*Within the apartment, Lindsay springs into excited action.*)

LINDSAY. Three buzzes—that's the signal! (*He herds Vera and Gooch out the door* D.R.) Come on—we're going to surprise her.

VERA. Oh, you're acting like a school boy. (*Lindsay comes back for Gooch, who has started toward the foyer door.*)

LINDSAY. You too! (*He pulls her off* R. *Patrick ushers Mame in, just as the others vanish. They are carrying parcels.*)

PATRICK. Welcome home, Auntie Mame. (*Auntie Mame looks about the room with a dramatic remoteness.*)

AUNTIE MAME. Dear old Beekman Place. It's so loyal. No matter how far I go, it just sits here and waits for me. You know, I rather expected Vera at the boat.

PATRICK. I wouldn't let her come. I wanted to be alone with you. (*They hug.*)

AUNTIE MAME. Patrick, my little Patrick. Now open your presents. Oh, Patrick, every time I see you, you get taller and more grown up. (*Patrick tears open a package and is baffled as he takes out a pair of Bavarian leather walking shorts. Auntie*

76

Mame holds them up against him. With a grin Patrick remembers a similar gift of many years before.)

PATRICK. Golly, short pants—at last! Can I try 'em on right now, Auntie Mame? Right now? (*They both laugh—but Auntie Mame's attitude changes instantly as Vera and Lindsay burst into the room. She drops the pants and strikes a mournful pose.*)

LINDSAY. Surprise! Surprise, Mame!

VERA. Surprise, darling—welcome home! (*Auntie Mame is now Duse, playing the Tragic Muse for the benefit of Vera.*)

AUNTIE MAME. (*Kissing Vera lightly on the cheek.*) Vera, dear. And staunch, stalwart Lindsay. How good of you both to rally 'round this bereft old woman. (*The others exchange glances.*)

PATRICK. Doesn't she look great?

LINDSAY. Mame, you look marvellous.

VERA. (*Eyeing the widow's weeds suspiciously.*) How can you tell? Mame, couldn't you have gone to *purple* by now?

LINDSAY. Mame, I haven't seen you since the Huns took Rome. Oh, no, it was when the Bears took Wall Street.

AUNTIE MAME. Oh, Lindsay, that day was Nirvana compared with what I've been through since. If only I'd jumped off the Matterhorn after him.

PATRICK. (*Crossing to the bar.*) Now, now, Auntie Mame— what you need is a good stiff drink.

AUNTIE MAME. No, no, no, Patrick. There is no barbiturate for my grief. I've given up alcohol completely. I haven't touched a drop since that St. Bernard brought me back to life. (*She becomes aware of the dictating machine and the typewriter.*) What's that?

LINDSAY. Well, that's your dictaphone and this is your typewriter. (*Gooch comes out of hiding and plods flat-footedly to her place at the desk. Auntie Mame looks at the secretary blankly.*)

AUNTIE MAME. And what's *that?*

GOOCH. I'm your "sponge"!

LINDSAY (*Clears his throat to spring his surprise.*) These are the tools of your new trade. You're going to write a book, Mame, and I'm going to publish it.

AUNTIE MAME. (*Waving away the paraphernalia, including*

77

Agnes.) Oh, Lindsay, don't be ridiculous. The way I feel, I can hardly read a book, let alone write one.

LINDSAY. (*Convincingly.*) All I want you to do is put your *self* on paper. Your memoirs.

PATRICK. Nobody's had a more exciting life than you, Auntie Mame. Done more things. I think it'd be terrific.

VERA. And think of all the fascinating people you've known. Like me.

LINDSAY. And it'll take your mind off things.

AUNTIE MAME. (*Suspiciously.*) Oh, I see—this is some kind of a conspiracy.

LINDSAY. No, no—

AUNTIE MAME. Some trumped-up occupational therapy, like leathercraft, or hooking rugs.

LINDSAY. I swear to you, it'll be a fascinating book. Why, it can easily be a best-seller. Mame, you'd be doing *me* a favor.

AUNTIE MAME. (*Starting to pace, intrigued.*) My memoirs. My memoirs. Patrick, you forgot my drink.

PATRICK. There's only Southern Comfort.

AUNTIE MAME. Anything, dear, just make it a double. (*She peels off some of the crepe, dumping it in Gooch's lap.*) What a lovely, lovely idea. I see it in two volumes, don't you, Lindsay? Boxed, like Proust.

LINDSAY. Let's get something to bind first. Remember, Mame, writing isn't easy—it means at least six months of gruelling concentration.

AUNTIE MAME. (*Her eyes lighting up.*) Let me see, let me see. (*Gooch takes her pad and poises her pencil like a female Boswell.*) "Chapter One, Page One!" (*Gooch writes furiously.*) Well, I'll be damned! This isn't so difficult, Lindsay. (*To Gooch, puzzled.*) What are you writing?

GOOCH. (*Reading back her shorthand by rote.*) "Chapter One, Page One, well, I'll be damned, this isn't so difficult, Lindsay, what are you writing."

VERA. She *is* fast.

PATRICK. (*Handing the drink to Mame.*) Atta girl, Auntie Mame —you're off and running.

AUNTIE MAME. (*To Patrick.*) Oh, Patrick, do you really think

I should? You heard Lindsay. After all, it'll take up all my time, and I really came home just to be with you.

PATRICK. You can't exactly be with me. No women allowed in the dorm.

AUNTIE MAME. I keep forgetting. You're all grown up now. You don't need me any more. (*Gooch is still taking every word down in frantic shorthand. Auntie Mame looks toward Lindsay.*) How do you turn her off? (*She resumes pacing.*) Now, where was I? The most important thing is to have a good beginning.

VERA. Is she supposed to start right this minute?

LINDSAY. Why don't you wait for your collaborator? He's on his way over here right now. (*There is a blank pause.*)

AUNTIE MAME. Collaborator?

LINDSAY. (*Backing water.*) Well, after all, you're only an ama— you're not a professional writer, and naturally I thought you'd want as much help as we could . . . (*Lindsay sees that this is completely the wrong tack. He puts on his most winning and gracious publisher's air.*) Mary Lord Bishop over at my office lined up this young man who's done a great deal of work with women authors, and . . .

AUNTIE MAME. (*With smoldering indignation.*) You don't trust me to write my own life myself! My God, who else could write it? (*She turns to Vera with a hollow laugh.*) He wants to give me a ghost!

LINDSAY. Not a ghost. More of an editor.

AUNTIE MAME. Who? Maxwell Perkins?

LINDSAY. Well, not quite. I haven't met this chap, O'Bannion, myself, but . . .

AUNTIE MAME. What did you say his name was?

LINDSAY. Brian O'Bannion. He's a . . .

AUNTIE MAME. O, God, deliver me. I can see him now—one of those beery, loose-mouthed Irish tenors.

LINDSAY. Mary says he's a very good poet. Wrote a volume called "The Wounded Tulip."

AUNTIE MAME. Probably pansy.

LINDSAY. Now, Mame.

AUNTIE MAME. Do you think I'm going to let some moon-eyed versifier mess up my memoirs with a lot of miserable Irish wit?

79

(*The doorbell buzzes. Patrick crosses to the foyer door and opens it. He converses in hushed tones with the visitor. Auntie Mame rails on against Lindsay and his editorial notions.*) I'll bet you don't give Willa Cather a low-comedy Irishman to tell her how to punctuate! Some funny-paper Jiggs out of Lady Gregory who . . .

PATRICK. Auntie Mame. There's a gentleman to see you. Mr. O'Bannion. (*Auntie Mame looks toward the doorway as O'Bannion enters. He is about thirty-five, tall, and very thin. He has a white skin and hair as black as coal—short and very curly. His eyes are turquoise-blue, rimmed with thick, black lashes. He wears a sportcoat of tweedy homespun with big suede patches at the elbows and a dirty trench coat is slung over his shoulder. O'Bannion shifts his weight gracefully in the doorway and gives Auntie Mame a slow, sad smile, parting a fine set of choppers. His intense blue eyes seem to reach out and caress her.*)

O'BANNION. (*Mellifously.*) Miss Bishop said it might not be amiss if I happened to drop by. (*O'Bannion half closes his eyes.*) You're Mrs. Burnside, of course. I could sense the aura of creative vitality about you. (*Vera, Lindsay and Gooch swing their respective gazes slowly from the newcomer to Auntie Mame.*)

AUNTIE MAME. (*Swallowing, a little flustered.*) Won't you come in, Mr. O'Bannion? We were just talking about you. (*He comes into the room like a graceful cat, slithering around the furniture with a kind of pelvis movement that is vaguely imitative of an electric eel. Lindsay, Vera and Gooch watch, fascinated by the crackling chemistry between O'Bannion and Auntie Mame.*) So awfully kind of you—a really renowned poet—to bother with my childish little scribblings. (*He gives her the old hot-eye again and she clears her throat nervously. As she crosses to him, she takes off her coat, dropping it behind her.*) Tell me, do you think that you and I can ever get any place? (*Quickly.*) With the book, I mean. (*O'Bannion takes Auntie Mame's hand in both of his and turns on that slow, sad smile again.*)

O'BANNION. I feel that you and I are going to create something beautiful! (*The Poet draws Auntie Mame closer to him, kissing her hand. She turns her back to the audience, and we see that her*) *"widow's weeds" are virtually backless; and somewhere around the fifth lumbar vertebra there is a livid heliotrope flower.)*

THE LIGHTS FADE

ACT II

SCENE 6

In the darkness we hear an ancient Gaelic lullaby, sung touchingly by unseen male voices.

VOICES. (*Off stage singing.*)
        "Tu ra loora lay,
        A loora lay,
        A toora loora lay;
        Tu ra loora lay,
        A loora lay,
        A toora loora lay."

The Beekman Place apartment—refurnished and refurbished as a literary atelier. The wall panels have been reversed, to become impressive bookcases. A bust of Dickens adorns the niche by the spiral staircase. Brian O'Bannion reclines on a leathery love-seat. To say he has made himself at home is a gross understatement; he is wearing a lush quilted dressing gown, and lounges with half-closed eyes, one forearm dramatically crooked over his meditative forehead.

Agnes Gooch sits like a flat-chested owl at her typewriter. Intensely she pounds away at a manuscript, the stethoscope of a dictaphone dangling from her ears. Apparently what she hears stirs the spirit of Prosperpine in her otherwise vacuous vitals. Occasionally a little "coo" of excitement escapes her lips, prompted by what is coming through the earphones. Her eyes sparkle and she types furiously with vicarious delight, jumping up and down with her feet under the desk.

O'BANNION. (*Annoyed.*) Please, please—Miss Gooch! How can I court the Muse with all that clackety-clackety?

81

GOOCH. I'm just taking off what Mrs. Burnside dictated. (*O'Bannion makes a deprecating gesture, waving aside anything that Auntie Mame has dictated as unimportant.*) But everything Mrs. Burnside dictates is so wonderful, it makes me all goose pimply. Why, when I listen to all the things she's done, and think of all the things I haven't done, I just want to go out and start trying everything and seeing everything and being everything—just like she has!

O'BANNION. I'm not sure the human race is ready for this book. (*Grandly.*) But it is *I* who shall clothe the naked incidents in poetry and symbolism. (*He glances at his watch, and calls off insolently.*) Norah! Ito! It's time for my nectar. (*Norah enters* U.C. *from the kitchen, her hands on her hips, and sizing up O'Bannion.*)

NORAH. What's that of yours it's time for, your majesty?

O'BANNION. My nectar, my nectar!

NORAH. (*Sarcastically.*) In exactly what part of Ireland is it, me bucko, where you drink "nectar"?

O'BANNION. (*Laying it on, airily.*) I come from that part of the Green Isle that has no latitude, nor longitude, and the leprechauns play in the twilight mist . . .

NORAH. You know, you're just about four bricks short of a full load! (*Norah goes off disgustedly. The telephone rings and Agnes answers it.*)

GOOCH. (*Into phone.*) Mrs. Burnside's residence. No, she isn't here—she's out on the moors. (*Pause.*) The moors. (*She listens again.*) Maybe you'd better talk with Mr. O'Bannion. (*Gooch gets up from her desk and carries the telephone on a long cord to the recumbent O'Bannion.*) It's that Mr. M. Lindsay Woolsey. He says it's important. (*Grandly O'Bannion takes the telephone from the servile secretary, who trembles with excitement at the instant their hands brush.*)

O'BANNION. (*Into phone.*) O'Bannion here. How are you, Lindsay? (*He listens.*) The moors? Oh that's what we call the terrace where I send her to meditate when the fog is crawling up from the Queensborough Bridge. (*He listens again.*) I can't put her on, but I'll be happy to give her another message. (*This probably nettles Lindsay, but O'Bannion continues with his atti-*

tude of bland mastery of the situation.) I'll tell her. But of course she'll be at your party tonight—I'm bringing her. Goldwyn? Samuel Goldwyn? (*He listens; this boy can smell a buck.*) Well, if he's interested, he'll have to buy our book sight unseen! (*He hangs up. Auntie Mame enters from R., looking like a Bronte with a long plaid muffler around her throat.*)

AUNTIE MAME. Oh, how the air of the moors releases the creative juices in the brain. Suddenly the fog lifted—and there was Welfare Island, looking for all the world like one magnificent peat bog.

O'BANNION. (*Eagerly.*) Alana, Samuel Goldwyn's coming to the party tonight. And we're to be at Lindsay's a half-hour early to tell him the story.

AUNTIE MAME. Dear Lindsay!—how good of him. Goldwyn's perfect for my story. After all, it *is* the American "Wuthering Heights." (*Gooch comes forward, apologizing for living. In one hand she has a stack of manuscript as thick as the New York telephone directory, and in the other hand she has two pages.*)

GOOCH. (*Indicating the thick sheaf of pages.*) Here's what you dictated, Mrs. Burnside . . . (*And indicating the two sheets*) . . . and here's what Mr. O'Bannion edited.

AUNTIE MAME. Oh. Thank you, Agnes. Now Mr. O'Bannion and I are going to work for a little bit. Why don't you do whatever it is you *do* do to relax?

GOOCH. Oh, thank you, Mrs. Burnside. I think I'll just fix myself a Dr. Pepper. (*Gooch takes a glass from the bar and goes off to the kitchen. She looks moon-eyed at O'Bannion as she exits. The moment she is gone, O'Bannion tries to nuzzle Auntie Mame, but deftly she slips away from his embrace.*)

O'BANNION. You glorious creature!

AUNTIE MAME. Brian—please—we're supposed to be working.

O'BANNION. Every time I come within ten feet of you, you reject me. How can we make music, until our lutes are in tune?

AUNTIE MAME. Well, after we finish the book, we can tune our lutes.

O'BANNION. We're not collaborating in the fullest sense of the word. (*Amorously.*) Alana, collaborate with me!

AUNTIE MAME. Brian, really!

O'BANNION. You're a block of ice, and we're supposed to be writing of burning passion and hot blood.

AUNTIE MAME. But I'm only eleven years of age in this part of the book.

O'BANNION. But *mature*—mature for eleven!

AUNTIE MAME. Brian, we've got to get to work.

O'BANNION. (*Sighs.*) All right, slave-driver. Where were we? (*Auntie Mame, relieved, examines the two pages which are the total of O'Bannion's editing.*)

AUNTIE MAME. Still on chapter two. It's not going very fast, is it? It took us a month-and-a-half on chapter one.

O'BANNION. But what a chapter.

AUNTIE MAME. What a month-and-a-half. (*Fending him off.*) Please, Brian, I cannot concentrate when you're doing things like that.

O'BANNION. Sorceress!

AUNTIE MAME. Besides, it takes Agnes no time at all to knock off a Dr. Pepper. (*Wishing the whole thing were over.*) How long do you think it's going to take us to finish the book?

O'BANNION. Flaubert spent thirteen years on "Madame Bovary."

AUNTIE MAME. How did she stand it?

O'BANNION. Read me our last sentence. (*Auntie Mame reaches for the top page on the thick stack of manuscript, and reads*)

AUNTIE MAME. (*Reading.*) "My puberty in Buffalo was drab."

O'BANNION. No, no! It has no majesty! "Drab" is such a drab word.

AUNTIE MAME. How right you are, Brian. It has no afflatus. (*Gooch enters from the kitchen, pouring a Dr. Pepper into a highball glass. Auntie Mame looks at her and gets an idea.*) What about "bleak"?

O'BANNION. (*Testing it.*) Bleak . . . bleak! How bleak was my puberty! Bleak Buffalo. Hear how those two words cling to each other—like a man and a woman, locked in each other's arms! Listen to the words sing!

GOOCH. (*Enraptured.*) How bleak was my puberty! (*Auntie Mame glares at Gooch, who melts away into the kitchen.*)

GOOCH. I'm sorry. (*As soon as Gooch is out of sight, O'Bannion goes to work again, kissing Auntie Mame helter-skelter.*)

O'BANNION. "Bleak." Oh, God, let me caress that talent! Where is it hidden, that germ of genius, *where* is it?

AUNTIE MAME. Brian, please— (*She glances at the page of edited manuscript.*) I'm worried about something. Coccamaura. I wonder if the general public is going to understand all this symbolism. (*She reads.*) "Like an echo from the caves of Cocca-maura, I came forth whilst Deirdre wept cool tears." Wouldn't it be simpler to say, "On the day I was born, it rained in Buffalo?"

O'BANNION. Drab, drab, drab!

AUNTIE MAME. It's drab, but it's clear.

O'BANNION. Clarity! How beauty is obscured by clarity.

AUNTIE MAME. All right, Brian, just what is it you want to say?

O'BANNION. (*Fumbling.*) Well, it's quite obvious— (*Suddenly he makes an extravagant gesture.*) We're drying up! We need inspiration! Get out the Yeats, the Synge, the Joyce! It's poetry time!

AUNTIE MAME. (*Wearily.*) Again??? (*Auntie Mame takes a thin volume from the table. Although she is bored with this poetry ritual, she accepts it as a part of the eccentric trappings of author-ship. Resignedly she slips to the floor with O'Bannion and they lie head to head, their feet extending in opposite directions. With dutiful concentration she begins to read.*)

> "The lyre and lute
> Are mute, are mute,
> And gray is the grave where my lover lies;
> Where my lover lies,
> Where my lover lies,
> Mute, mute, mute."

(*Gooch comes from the kitchen, stepping over them.*)

GOOCH. I rinsed out the glass.

AUNTIE MAME. Aren't you neat, Agnes? (*Gooch plods back into the kitchen.*)

O'BANNION. Glorious! Glorious! More! More! (*Auntie Mame turns to another poem. Patrick appears in the hallway and lets himself in. Auntie Mame and O'Bannion are so wrapped up in their "work" that they do not hear the sound of Patrick coming in. She reads.*)

AUNTIE MAME.

> "Bright bleeds the blood of the broken rose,
> And my loins leap up to utter passion's feckless cry.
> My loins cry out for thee,
> O love!
> O love!—"

(*O'Bannion has been acting out the imagery on Auntie Mame's neck and ear; Patrick clears his throat.*) Oh, hush, Agnes.

PATRICK. (*Cooly.*) Auntie Mame—(*Auntie Mame and O'Bannion spring up from the floor. Auntie Mame is a little flustered.*)

AUNTIE MAME. Why, Patrick—what are you doing home from school?

PATRICK. I had something very important I wanted to talk with you about—but if you're busy . . .

AUNTIE MAME (*Covering quickly.*) Oh, Brian and I were just working—on the book.

PATRICK. I'll bet that's going to be some book.

AUNTIE MAME. This is my nephew, Patrick; this is my collaborator, Mr. Brian O'Bannion. (*The two nod to each other with the cordiality of Ben Gurion encountering Nasser.*)

PATRICK. (*Glumly.*) We've met. Auntie Mame, I wonder if I could talk to you a little bit—alone. It's rather personal—and rather important.

AUNTIE MAME. Why, of course, my dear. If you don't mind, Brian—? (*O'Bannion, somewhat wounded, decides to make an exit.*)

O'BANNION. (*Starting up the staircase.*) It's quite all right. I was just going up to my room—to change. (*Raising his voice.*) Pay no attention to me. Don't anybody pay any attention to me at all! (*He exits grandly up the stairs.*)

PATRICK. To his *room!* Is he *living* here?

AUNTIE MAME. Why, of course, darling. There was nobody in the sculpture room. And since we're working together literally day and night—so to speak . . .

PATRICK. (*Primly.*) It looks very cozy.

AUNTIE MAME. For a moment there you sounded exactly like somebody from the Knickerbocker Bank.

PATRICK. Please get O'Bannion out of here. Right away.

AUNTIE MAME. I beg your pardon?

PATRICK. I don't want him in this house.

AUNTIE MAME. Aren't you taking a rather imperious tone? Mr. O'Bannion is my colleague.

PATRICK. Colleague, my foot! Gloria would never understand that you and this Irish phoney are . . .

AUNTIE MAME. Gloria? Who's Gloria? (*Patrick takes a deep breath.*)

PATRICK. Auntie Mame, listen to me. (*He takes her shoulders.*) I've met a girl. I've been going with her for several months.

AUNTIE MAME. Oh?

PATRICK. She's—well, she's a very special girl. I guess I should have told you about her before. I would have, but I knew you were all tied up with your book and . . . (*Significantly.*) . . . everything. And until now, it wasn't really definite.

AUNTIE MAME. What's definite now?

PATRICK. Gloria's *the* girl, that's what's definite. And you're going to meet her. Tonight.

AUNTIE MAME. I hope you didn't leave her sitting in the car.

PATRICK. I dropped her off at her girl friend's. Bunny Bixler's on Park Avenue. She wanted to get spruced up before she met you.

AUNTIE MAME. (*Nervously.*) Well—I'd better do some sprucing up of my own.

PATRICK. (*Staring toward the foyer door.*) I'll bring Gloria back in about ten or fifteen minutes, okay?

AUNTIE MAME. (*A little flustered.*) I'll have my face all organized. (*From off, we hear O'Bannion's voice at the top of the stairs.*)

O'BANNION. (*Calling.*) Mame, where did Ito hide my white tie? (*Patrick stops dead in his tracks, pointing his finger toward the sound of the voice.*)

PATRICK. Wait a minute. If *he's* still in the house, I'm not going to bring Gloria back here.

AUNTIE MAME. May I inquire why?

PATRICK. Gloria happens to be a very sensitive and well-brought up girl. And I don't want you flaunting your new flames and your old pecadillocs in front of her.

AUNTIE MAME. (*Freezing.*) Then why bring her here at all?

PATRICK. (*Getting angry himself.*) You want to know the truth? I've been trying to avoid it. But she wanted to meet you.

AUNTIE MAME. So you just dropped by to make sure I was all scrubbed up and presentable for inspection! Is that it?

PATRICK. (*Suffering.*) No, no, Auntie Mame. (*Pleading.*) Just for five minutes tonight will you try to act like a normal human being? Then I won't make any more demands on you. Gloria's from good stock—and she just doesn't have to know about all your airy-fairy friends from Fire Island; or your Irish friend upstairs. I'd just rather my little Glory didn't know about a lot of things that ordinary mortals simply don't have to know about. (*There is a deathly pause.*)

AUNTIE MAME. (*With quiet intensity.*) Should she know that I think you've turned into one of the most beastly, bourgeois, babbity little snobs on the Eastern seaboard,—or will you be able to make that quite clear, without any help from me? (*This is the first time in Patrick's entire life that Auntie Mame has really let him have it with both barrels. He is stunned. He looks at her for a moment, then turns on his heels and starts out.*)

PATRICK. All right. Just forget about the whole thing. (*Auntie Mame realizes it would be fatal to let him go out in this mood.*)

AUNTIE MAME. Patrick—bring your girl here. I won't let her get the wrong impression, I promise. (*They look at each other.*)

PATRICK. (*With a warm smile.*) Thanks, Auntie Mame. (*He goes out. Auntie Mame begins to pace, chewing on the knuckle of her index finger. From upstairs we hear O'Bannion's untrained Irish baritone singing, "I'll Take You Home Again, Kathleen." At this sound, Auntie Mame really looks worried: how is she going to get him out of here?*)

AUNTIE MAME. (*Calling up the stairs.*) Brian . . . (*O'Bannion breaks off in mid-song, and appears at the head of the stairs in full dress shirt and trousers—but no tie or coat yet.*)

O'BANNION. (*From the head of the stairs.*) Yes, Alana? Why aren't you getting dressed? We can't keep the Goldwyns waiting.

AUNTIE MAME. (*With difficulty.*) Would you mind awfully if I didn't go to the party with you tonight?

O'BANNION. (*Affronted.*) You want me to go *alone?* I wouldn't think of it!

AUNTIE MAME. But—something came up . . .

O'BANNION. (*Imperiously.*) Hurry and get dressed, Alana. I'm *not* goin' to that party alone! (*He turns on his heel and goes back into his upstairs bedroom. Gooch plods out of the kitchen and whines at Auntie Mame.*)

GOOCH. Mrs. Burnside, if there's nothing else you wanted me for, I just thought I'd turn in.

AUNTIE MAME. Agnes, I wonder— (*Auntie Mame starts pacing around Agnes.*)

GOOCH. (*Getting nervous at Auntie Mame's perusal.*) Mrs. Burnside, is anything wrong?

AUNTIE MAME. Agnes! You're coming out.

GOOCH. (*Clutching the sides of her dress.*) Where?

AUNTIE MAME. (*Yanking off Agnes' glasses.*) Why, Agnes, you have lovely eyes. Take those glasses off and leave them off *forever.*

GOOCH. But I can't see anything out of my right eye.

AUNTIE MAME. Then look out of the left one. (*Auntie Mame points to Agnes' shoes.*) What do you call those things?

GOOCH. Orthopedic oxfords.

AUNTIE MAME. Kick 'em off! (*Gooch, baffled, complies. Auntie Mame pulls her dress tight around the midriff.*) My goodness, Agnes—you do have a bust. Where on earth have you been hiding it all these months?

GOOCH. (*Getting worried.*) Mrs. Burnside—

AUNTIE MAME. (*Positively.*) Take off your clothes.

GOOCH. (*With a proper little gasp.*) Mrs. Burnside! There's a man in the house!

AUNTIE MAME. Don't be a goose, Agnes, get those clothes off and keep them off. (*Agnes peels out of her clothes and stands trembling in a shapeless white slip. Mame calls off.*) Norah! Ito! Come on in here, we've got some work to do! (*Norah and Ito hurry in from the kitchen.*)

GOOCH. (*Cringing.*) I don't have a very clear picture of what's going on.

AUNTIE MAME. (*Briskly.*) Agnes, I'm sending you to that party tonight with Mr. O'Bannion. (*Gooch looks thunder-struck and begins to get the shakes.*)

GOOCH. Oh, I couldn't. I'm too nervous. (*Auntie Mame strides to the bar and pours a stiff slug of Irish whiskey for Agnes.*)

AUNTIE MAME. This'll calm you down.

GOOCH. But spirits do the most terrible thing to me. I'm not the same girl.

AUNTIE MAME. What's wrong with that? (*She forces the jigger on Gooch. The Secretary starts to drink, then hesitates.*)

GOOCH. Will it mix with Dr. Pepper?

AUNTIE MAME. (*Emphatically.*) He'll love it. Drink! (*Agnes drinks. Before the liquor hits bottom, Auntie Mame is slapping Agnes' cheeks.*) Oh, Agnes, for God's sake, close your pores! We really should do something about that skin. A good physic would work wonders, but I guess it's too late in the day to start that. (*She turns crisply to the servants.*) Norah, go upstairs, drag out that sexy Patou velvet! Ito, get out all my cosmetics: the face creams, the lipsticks, the eyebrow pencils! (*Ito scampers up the stairs delightedly.*)

ITO. You see, me be Charlie of the Ritz! (*Auntie Mame starts to drag Agnes up the stairs, but Agnes hangs back, holding onto the bannister.*)

GOOCH. (*A coward to the core.*) Mrs. Burnside, I think I know what you want me to do, and I'm not a bit sure I want to do it! (*Norah is behind Agnes, pushing her up the stairs; and Auntie Mame is tugging at her from above.*)

AUNTIE MAME. Agnes, where's your *spine*? Here you've been taking my dictation all these weeks, and you don't get the message of my book! Live!—that's the message!

GOOCH. (*Still hanging back, as if she didn't know what the word meant.*) Live?

AUNTIE MAME. Yes! Life is a banquet, and most poor sons-of-bitches are *starving* to death! Live! (*Intoxicated, partly by the liquor, partly by Auntie Mame's enthusiasm, Agnes decides to let herself go as she charges up the stairs.*)

GOOCH. (*Hypnotized.*) Live! Live! Live! (*The lights fade.*)

ACT II

Scene 7

Scene: The Beekman Place Apartment, a half hour later.
As the lights come up, the room is empty. Then Ito scampers down the spiral stairs, giggling giddily. He disappears into the kitchen.
Next Norah hurries down the stairs, gathering up some of Gooch's discarded clothing.

NORAH. (*Muttering.*) The whole house has gone nuts. (*Shaking her head as she goes off.*) She'll never make a silk purse out of *that* sow's ear! (*Now Auntie Mame appears at the head of the stairs. She turns back as Agnes calls to her from off.*)
GOOCH'S VOICE. (*Calling from off.*) Mrs. Burnside, I can't breathe!
AUNTIE MAME. Fine! If you can breathe, it isn't tight enough. (*Auntie Mame starts down the stairs, carrying a fur wrap. She looks at her watch. Under her breath:*) Oh, God. (*Glancing nervously toward the outside door, she takes several glasses toward the bar, straightening up for Gloria's imminent arrival. In the manner of a grand duke, O'Bannion comes down the stairs in his full dress regalia.*)
O'BANNION. (*Startled.*) And why aren't you ready?
AUNTIE MAME. (*Turning to face O'Bannion.*) Now, Brian, you're going to have to understand. I'm not going to the party tonight.
O'BANNION. (*Splenetically.*) Then *I'm* not going either! (*Stamping his foot.*) I'm not, I'm not, I'm *not!*
AUNTIE MAME. You can use the Dusenberg. And I've got a date for you!
O'BANNION. Who? (*Slightly mollified.*) Vera?
AUNTIE MAME. Certainly not. You couldn't trust Vera. (*Going to the foot of the stairs and calling up.*) Agnes—?

91

O'BANNION. Agnes! You certainly can't expect me to be seen at a fashionable party with that—(*Haughtily.*) Would you ask Toscanini to lead a harmonica band? I'm staying right here!

AUNTIE MAME. Now, Brian.

O'BANNION. You don't appreciate me. I'm a minstrel without a lute—

AUNTIE MAME. Not those lutes again.

O'BANNION. (*Throwing himself on the sofa and kicking his heels like a petulant infant.*) I won't take Agnes to the party! I won't, I won't, I won't, I won't. (*Gooch starts down the stairs.*)

AUNTIE MAME. (*Coaching.*) Head up! Shoulders back! Tummy in! That's right! Tonight, Agnes, you're the Queen of Rumania! (*Gooch looks almost regal. O'Bannion's jaw drops.*)

O'BANNION. Well! (*O'Bannion gives her the old hot-eye; then offers Gooch his arm, and she takes it.*)

GOOCH. (*Transported.*) Hotcha. (*In the outer hallway, Patrick and Gloria appear. Patrick starts to use his key to let himself in, then thinks better of it and presses the door buzzer. Auntie Mame jumps.*)

AUNTIE MAME. Quick, Brian. Hang those furs on the Gooch. Hurry! (*She hesitates for a moment, then crosses to the door with some misgivings. She opens the door and greets Patrick and Gloria.*)

PATRICK. (*As if he were presenting the Kimberly diamond.*) Auntie Mame, this is Gloria. Gloria Upson. And this is my Auntie Mame. Mrs. Burnside.

GLORIA. (*Extending a limp hand.*) I cahn't tell you how pleased I am to make your acquaintance. (*Gloria is lovely, tanned, pleasant, but without real warmth. There is something wrong with this girl—you can't quite put your finger on it—a kind of ersatz composure, a mail-order chic. When she talks, there seems to be novocaine in her upper lip.*)

AUNTIE MAME. Come in, children, come in. There are some friends here I want you to meet.

PATRICK. (*Bristling.*) Auntie Mame, you promised—(*But Auntie Mame is completely composed as she ushers them into the living room.*)

AUNTIE MAME. This is my secretary, Miss Gooch. My good right

hand, my Boswell, you might say. (*With an appropriate gesture.*)
This is Miss Upson, and my nephew Patrick. (*Gooch's eyes light
up at the sight of Patrick.*)

GOOCH. Oh, can this be the helpless little infant you found in a
basket on your doorstep?

AUNTIE MAME. (*Indicating the resplendent O'Bannion.*) And
this is Agnes' *date*. What's your boy-friend's name, Agnes?
O'Bannion, wasn't it? (*Patrick breathes a sigh of relief at his
aunt's deft recovery.*)

O'BANNION. (*Curtly.*) We'll be on our way. Good night.

GLORIA. I cahn't tell you how pleased I am to have made your
acquaintance, Mr. O'Bannion. (*Turning to Gooch.*) And Miss
Boswell. (*O'Bannion and Gooch go out.*)

AUNTIE MAME. (*Taking Gloria's hands.*) Patrick says you're
very special to him; that means you're very special to me, too.

GLORIA. (*Looking about, vacuously.*) My! What a stunning
apartment. Don't tell me you're read all these books, Mrs. Burnside!

AUNTIE MAME. Well, not all of them. Do sit down, dear. Can
I get you something? A cognac, or a Drambuie—

PATRICK. Would you like another hot chocolate, honey?

GLORIA. Oh, not a *thing*. On our way to Bunny's, Patrick and I
just stuffed ourselves at Howard Johnson's. (*Gloria laughs
musically.*) And do you know what your silly nephew did? He
talked French to the waiter. Imagine anybody talking French to a
waiter at a Howard Johnson's! (*She nudges him playfully.*)
Show-off.

AUNTIE MAME. If nobody minds, I think *I'll* have something.
(*She pours herself a brandy; her face is troubled by her first
appraisal of the girl—but she's determined to keep an open mind.*)
You're at school, dear?

GLORIA. I'm an Upper-Richmond Girls School girl.

AUNTIE MAME. How did you get that lovely tan so early in
spring?

GLORIA. Oh, I played hookey for a couple of weeks. Mums and
Daddums and I went down to our place in Fort Lauderdale. We
have a place in Fort Lauderdale.

PATRICK. While she was gone, it was the longest two weeks in my life. And yet—it's the funniest thing, Auntie Mame—when Gloria and I are together, we don't really do much of anything. I mean, we don't even talk—I'm just so busy staring at her.

GLORIA. Silly.

AUNTIE MAME. Have you chosen your major yet, dear?

GLORIA. (*Blankly.*) Chosen my major?

AUNTIE MAME. What courses are you taking at college?

GLORIA. Oh, just a general sort of liberal arts thing. You know, English Lit and like that. Upper Richmond's top-hole. Really top-hole.

AUNTIE MAME. How did you two ever get acquainted?

GLORIA. Oh, Uncle Dwight introduced us.

AUNTIE MAME. Uncle Dwight?

PATRICK. That's Mr. Babcock.

AUNTIE MAME. Oh, yes.

GLORIA. He's not really my uncle. But he's been a real close friend of the family ever since I was a little girl with braces on my teeth.

AUNTIE MAME. Someday I'd like to meet "Mums and Dad-dums."

PATRICK. Oh, we don't want to bother you with a lot of family stuff.

GLORIA. Naturally, we'll expect you at the wedding.

AUNTIE MAME. (*Pale.*) The wedding?

PATRICK. I told you it was definite, Auntie Mame.

GLORIA. We've decided on a September wedding. It's lovely, just lovely then at the Church of the Heavenly Rest—that's right near our place in Mountebank.

AUNTIE MAME. September. Dear me. Tell me,—just where is Mountebank.

GLORIA. Right above Darien. You'll love it. It's the most re-stricted community in our part of Connecticut.

AUNTIE MAME. I'll get a blood test. (*Patrick knows a storm cloud when he sees one, and he's determined to get his girl out before the downpour.*)

PATRICK. If we hurry, we could still catch the last couple of dances at the country club.

AUNTIE MAME. I hate to have you rush off. (*But Gloria doesn't care about sticking around here; she smiles synthetically, and stiff-arms a handshake.*)

GLORIA. I cahn't tell you how pleased I am to have made your acquaintance.

PATRICK. (*Halfway to the door.*) I'll drop you a note and let you know what's happening.

AUNTIE MAME. Do that! (*Gloria goes out, Patrick turns.*)

PATRICK. (*Lowering his voice.*) Isn't she a dream?

AUNTIE MAME. Oh, yes—yes, she is . . . Did I pass inspection?

PATRICK. You were great, Auntie Mame. Really top-hole. (*Patrick goes out. Auntie Mame stands alone, a little dazed—and not at all sure that what has just happened has really happened.*)

AUNTIE MAME. (*With a semi-bitter bemusement.*) Why did I ever buy him those long pants?

THE LIGHTS FADE

ACT II

Scene 8

Scene: The Beekman Place apartment again; no changes. The lighting indicates that it is early morning of the following day. Norah comes downstairs, carrying a breakfast tray containing juice and a raw egg in an egg cup.

Ito, in a chauffeur's uniform, hurries on from the D.L. door. They meet in the center of the apartment.

ITO. (*Confused.*) Missy say go to garage, get Dusenberg—we drive to Connecticut today—very important. I go to garage. No Dusenberg.

NORAH. And it's his majesty's breakfast I've got here. Only there's not a smell of that O'Bannion in the place. You suppose he's gone for good, God bless the day?

ITO. Me no know what to do. Got road map to Mountebank. Got uniform. No Dusenberg.

NORAH. That Mr. Lindsay always has a car or two. (*She hands Ito the egg cup.*) The glorious thing is that O'Bannion's gone. You can have his raw egg. I'll drink his nectar. (*But they stop abruptly as Gooch staggers on from outside. The strap of her evening dress is askew, her hair is tangled and she has a definite "out-all-night" air about her.*)

ITO. What happen, Missy Gooch?

GOOCH. I *lived*! (*She seems hypnotized as she walks straight across stage.*)

NORAH. What kind of a party was that?

GOOCH. Oh, we never got to that party. Brian said he was going to take me for a drive. But we parked.

ITO. Where Dusenberg now, Missy Gooch?

GOOCH. Brian dropped me off here—and said he was driving due west. (*Looks around, panicky.*) Where's Mrs. Burnside?

ITO. She put on face—get ready for trip to Connecticut.

GOCH. I've got to see her before she goes.

NORAH. Is anything wrong, Miss Gooch?

GOOCH. I did just what she told me. I lived! I've got to find out what to do *now*!!! (*Ito and Norah look at each other significantly, as Gooch shuffles off. The lights fade.*)

ACT II

Scene 9

Scene: The patio of the Upsons' home in Montebank. Late afternoon.

This, for this version, should be in one, before the neutral-drop. A portable-roll-on bar is L. *A bench, also on wheels, is center, backed-up by an early-American wagonwheel. Before the lights come up, the prattle of extroverted chickadees informs us that we have reached the apotheosis of exurbia. The sunlight of a late spring afternoon slants across the little flagstone heaven where the Upsons take their ease. Mr. Upson is carrying out the bar stools—Early American; and Mrs. Upson enters with trays of*

96

hors d'oeuvres—also Early American, which she places on a table.
The Upsons are a hearty, well-padded couple, enormously pleased
with themselves and their way of life.

MRS. UPSON. Well, I just think it's a very good match for our
little Gloria, that's what I think. (*Mrs. Upson is fluttering ner-
vously about, prettying up the patio. She is a rosy, flaccid woman
who thinks Walter Lippman makes tea. Mr. Upson is loud and
square as the basement of a Masonic Temple. He thinks Walter
Lippman is a Socialist.*)
MR. UPSON. (*Lifting up his paraphernalia on the bar.*) I still
can't see why Dwight didn't want us to meet the aunt.
MRS. UPSON. I guess we never would have if she hadn't phoned.
I thought it was only my duty to ask her to buzz up here. Besides,
I was dying to get a look at her.
MR. UPSON. Where is she now?
MRS. UPSON. She's up in the guest-room changing again.
MR. UPSON. She certainly brought enough clothes.
MRS. UPSON. And they're expensive ones, Claude. I looked at
the labels.
MR. UPSON. Why, I'll bet she's even better fixed than Dwight
figured. (*Mrs. Upson purses her lips, a little worried.*)
MRS. UPSON. I hope it's all right to have the cocktail hour here
on the patio. I don't want her to think we live like gypsies.
MR. UPSON. You show me a gypsy that lives like we do. (*He
chortles with self-satisfaction.*)
MRS. UPSON. Now, Claude Upson, you be *genteel* in front of
Mrs. Burnside!
MR. UPSON. (*Belligerently.*) God damn it, I'm always genteel!
(*From inside the house, we hear Auntie Mame call out in her
most Connecticut manner.*)
AUNTIE MAME'S VOICE. (*From off.*) Yoo-hoo!
MRS. UPSON. Oh, that must be she. (*She raises her voice.*)
We're out here on the patio, Mrs. Burnside. (*Auntie Mame, stun-
ningly dressed for spring-in-the-country, starts through the door-
way onto the patio, but suddenly loses footing.*)
AUNTIE MAME. Oops! (*The Upsons react with concern.*) Oh
dear—I'm always tripping over that *adorable* little hooked rug.

MRS. UPSON. Do be careful; we'd feel awful if you had an accident.

MR. UPSON. (*Jovially.*) Don't you worry. I've got plenty of personal liability insurance.

AUNTIE MAME. (*Blithely.*) Well, then let's bring on more hooked rugs!

MR. UPSON. Now, there's one thing we oughta know right off. You do take a little nip now and then?

AUNTIE MAME. (*Smiling prettily.*) On festive occasions.

MR. UPSON. (*Blandly.*) Good, I'll have an Upson daiquiri ready in a minute. (*Auntie Mame would rather have vermouth and Castoria, but she indicates her pleasure at the prospect.*)

AUNTIE MAME. (*Glancing around the patio.*) Oh, Mrs. Upson, I can't get over how much thought you've given every detail of your house.

MRS. UPSON. We've done everything we could to make it seem like a little bit of authentic Colonial America.

AUNTIE MAME. And how well you've succeeded! Those adorable miniatures in the powder room of John Quincy Adams.

MRS. UPSON. Well, I said to the decorator from Altman's—

AUNTIE MAME. Altman's? I would have said Sloane's. Solid Sloane's!

MRS. UPSON. (*Giggling.*) Don't you have an *eye*, though. *Downstairs* is Sloane's. Upstairs is Altman's!

MR. UPSON. (*Looking up from his bar chores.*) I'll bet you didn't notice our sign-post out by the driveway . . .?

AUNTIE MAME. But I *did*! I did! What a divine name you've chosen for your place. (*Trying to recall.*) "Upson . . ."

UPSONS. (*Together.*) "Downs!"

AUNTIE MAME. I'll bet *you* thought that up, Mrs. Upson.

MRS. UPSON. Oh, no. It was Claude. I'm just a homebody. Claude's the clever one. (*Mr. Upson laughs.*) I'm so delighted to see we have the same tastes. I know you're just going to adore the wedding we've planned for the children.

AUNTIE MAME. (*Wetting her lips.*) Now, about the wedding. Don't you think, Mrs. Upson, that . . .

MR. UPSON. Hold it! Hold it! Let's forget the last names right off. After all, we're practically family, aren't we? I just want to be plain Claude.

MRS. UPSON. And I'm Doris.

AUNTIE MAME. "Doris." I've always loved the name of Doris. Not too coy and not too chic. Sort of bitter-sweet.

MR. UPSON. What do we call you?

AUNTIE MAME. All my intimate friends call me just plain Mame.

MRS. UPSON. How lovely. (*Trying to get on Auntie Mame's level.*) Old-fashioned—and yet modern, too. Mamie.

AUNTIE MAME. (*correcting.*) Mame.

MR. UPSON. (*Pouring a daiquiri, and handing it to her.*) Well, Mamie old girl, here's your poison. I make my daiquiris with a secret ingredient I learned from this native down in Havana, Cuba. You'll never guess what the secret ingredient is—but I'll say *this* much. There's no sugar in a Claude Upson daiquiri. (*She sips it.*)

AUNTIE MAME. And yet it's so *sweet*. What *ever* do you use? Chocolate ice cream?

MR. UPSON. (*Guffawing.*) Sa-a-y, that's rich. Did you hear that, Doris? Chocolate ice cream. (*He puts a bear-like hand on Auntie Mame's shoulder.*) Since we're practically relatives, I'm going to let you in on my little secret, *honey*.

AUNTIE MAME. I beg your pardon?

MR. UPSON. Strained honey—that's the secret ingredient. (*He chortles.*) Of course, I use quite a little rum, too! (*Mame points playfully into her glass and in a hail-fellow-well-met mood. Mrs. Upson goes to table and comes over with trays of canapes.*)

MRS. UPSON. Now, I made these especially for you, dear.

AUNTIE MAME. (*Taking a canape.*) Don't they look delicious, though. Mm-m-m-mm-mm-*mm*! (*She takes a bite.*) What *are* they?

MRS. UPSON. Well, I take two cans of tuna fish and put them through the meat-grinder, then add clam juice and peanut butter. It's a recipe I cut out of the "Ladies Home Journal." (*She proffers the other tray.*) These others are just plain jack cheese and chutney. (*Mrs. Upson steers Auntie Mame to a bench. Surreptitiously, Mame tosses the hors d'oeuvre over the patio wall.*) Now,

sit you down right here, Mamie. There's something *special* I have to show you. (*She deposits trays and pulls out a photo album.*)
AUNTIE MAME. (*Gleefully.*) Baby pictures. Of Gloria?
MRS. UPSON. Oh, the whole family, more or less. (*They start to leaf through the album.*)
AUNTIE MAME. (*Pointing to one snap.*) On a bear rug! Isn't that precious? (*Mame tosses her drink over her shoulder when Mrs. Upson isn't looking.*)
MRS. UPSON. (*Giggling.*) Better not ever let Patrick see *that* one! That's Miss Tuthill—little Glory's first school teacher. I think the light was hurting her eyes. (*She turns another page.*) And here's Gloria when she was a flower girl at Muriel Puce's wedding.
AUNTIE MAME. What's she eating?
MRS. UPSON. Oh, those are the braces on her teeth.
MR. UPSON. All right, all right—that's enough of the girly-girly talk. I figure while we've got Mamie here, we oughta tell her what the plans are. (*He sits beside Mame, his fat paw around her shoulder.*)
AUNTIE MAME. Plans?
MR. UPSON. For Patrick's career. Dwight Babcock and I have it all worked out. He came to me, and he said "Claude"—he always calls me Claude—
MRS. UPSON. (*Confidentially to Auntie Mame, crowding her from the opposite side.*) When they're together, it's "Dwight and Claude, Claude and Dwight"—that's all you hear.
MR. UPSON. Yup! Yup! Yup! Now, when the kiddies get back from their honeymoon, I want Patrick to take his choice. With my connections, I can slip him into a berth on Madison Avenue, or a seat on the Stock Exchange.
AUNTIE MAME. A seat *and* a berth!—(*Auntie Mame practically bumps noses with Mrs. Upson. Mr. Upson notices her glass is empty.*)
MR. UPSON. Say, you're a fast drinker, Mamie! But don't you worry—I made plenty.
AUNTIE MAME. Oh, I don't think—(*Upson takes her glass and crosses to the bar.*)
MRS. UPSON. You don't happen to like gin, do you, Mamie?

AUNTIE MAME. (*whispers.*) I adore it.

MRS. UPSON. After dinner, I'll get the cards and we'll have a little game.

MR. UPSON. Now, we come to the problem of what to give the kiddies for a wedding present. And I've got that all settled, too. Here's my idea, Mamie. Why don't we get together, you and I, and buy the newlyweds *that*! (*He stares dead-front. Auntie Mame follows his gaze, but doesn't see anything.*)

AUNTIE MAME. What?

MR. UPSON. (*He takes her arm and leads her* D.C.) Why, that lot—right next door. Wouldn't that make a wedding present, though? We could take down this wall here so that their patio would come smack up against ours. You couldn't tell where one left off and the other began!

AUNTIE MAME. So you wouldn't really be losing a daughter: you'd be gaining a patio!

MR. UPSON. But we've got to move fast. Some people are bidding on that property. (*He lowers his voice.*) The *wrong* kind.

AUNTIE MAME. Oh?

MR. UPSON. Fella named Epstein. A-bra-ham Epstein.

AUNTIE MAME. (*Enthusing.*) The cellist? How lucky you are. All that lovely music right next door! And she's a darling. One of the nicest —

MRS. UPSON. (*Confidentially.*) I guess maybe you don't understand quite how it *is* up here, Mamie. But this section is restricted only to our property line. So we feel we have an obligation to make sure that—well—*you* know.

MR. UPSON. Tell you what I'll do, Mamie. I'll have my broker make a bid—and when it goes in escrow we'll just divvy it up, fifty-fifty. You won't have to worry about a thing. (*Auntie Mame plants her glass on the bar with an irritated precision that is only a hint of the emotion repressed within her.*)

AUNTIE MAME. (*Too quietly.*) My, you've thought of everything, haven't you! Laid out Patrick's career—planned the wedding—even chosen my wedding gift. Well, I guess there's only one thing left for me to do. (*She crosses back between the Upsons.*)

MR. UPSON. What's that, Mamie?

AUNTIE MAME. Give an intimate little family dinner! (*Auntie Mame looks archly from one to the other, the lights begin to fade.*)
MRS. UPSON. Lovely, lovely.
MR. UPSON. Mamie, you're top hole! (*The lights are out.*)

ACT II

Scene 10

Scene: The Beekman Place Apartment. The room is undergoing another metamorphosis, and any previous decor would seem definitely mid-Victorian. The panels have been reversed to display some Fauvist outrages. The furniture looks like a geometrist's nightmare. But presiding over this transformation is a trim red-head named Pegeen Ryan, who is crisp and businesslike as she arranges the abstract ashtrays and the Twenty-First-Century objets d'art.
At first, Pegeen is bustling about the apartment alone. Then Agnes Gooch enters from right. She, too, has been transformed by the miracle of maternity. There is no doubt about it; the Gooch is six months pregnant. Her pelvis protests at every step as she crosses wordlessly to the kitchen. Neither Gooch nor Pegeen pays the slightest attention to the other. Gooch goes off. Patrick, in dinner dress, appears in the foyer and lets himself in. His nervousness gives way to amazement as he enters and takes in the new decor.

PATRICK. What's going on?
PEGEEN. Face-lifting. (*She sizes up Patrick, not uncritically.*) You must be the heir-apparent. The "Little Love."
PATRICK. (*Wandering around the room.*) Are you the new decorator? Did you do all this?
PEGEEN. (*Grins.*) For money. (*Ito enters in livery, carrying the bare skeleton of a futuristic sofa.*) Right here, Ito. That's fine. (*Ito puts down the sofa at Pegeen's direction.*)

PATRICK. What are you made up for, Ito? Where's my aunt?

ITO. Missee dress now. (*Ito goes off to kitchen. Pegeen gathers up some cushions and places them on the bench, which is just a few inches from the floor.*)

PATRICK. What's that?

PEGEEN. It's a sofa. Danish Modern. You find it every place except Denmark. Your aunt made it very explicit: she said she didn't want a sofa that sat around singing "Nearer My God To Thee."

PATRICK. Yeah, but do *you* like it?

PEGEEN. She's not paying me to like it. If she told me she wanted a tombstone for a coffee table, I'd get her a tombstone for a coffee table. And it would be a *good* tombstone. But that doesn't mean I'm going out and buy one for myself.

PATRICK. You should have told my aunt that.

PEGEEN. I did.

PATRICK. You know, you're the first *honest* interior decorator she's ever had, Miss - - - ?

PEGEEN. Pegeen Ryan. Unincorporated.

PATRICK. (*Shaking her hand, pleasantly.*) Hi.

PEGEEN. Hi. (*But Patrick is restless again. He glances toward the head of the stairs.*)

PATRICK. Where is she? Where's my aunt?

PEGEEN. You already asked that.

PATRICK. Did I?

PEGEEN. Relax. People get married every day.

PATRICK. (*Nervously.*) I'm not getting married every day. I'm getting married three weeks from Tuesday.

PEGEEN. (*Tossing it off.*) Congratulations.

AUNTIE MAME. Patrick—! (*He turns and sees Auntie Mame starting down the stairs. She is really dressed to the hilt, in a gold hostess gown. Both she and Patrick start speaking at once.*)

PATRICK. Auntie Mame, what's the idea of all this?

AUNTIE MAME. (*Anticipating his protest.*) Now, Patrick, I don't want to hear a word out of you. I simply had to drive up to Mountebank. Doris insisted!

PATRICK. Oh, that part's all right—they adore you. (*Casting a*

103

dubious eye around the room.) But why did you have to change—?

AUNTIE MAME. (*Innocently.*) Really, I'm so relieved. Now, I've tried to make everything special for tonight, and to give the Upsons as cozy a time as they gave me. (*Patrick nods vaguely.*)

PEGEEN. (*Suddenly.*) Oh! I forgot the horror! (*Pegeen darts off R., but Auntie Mame calls after her.*)

AUNTIE MAME. Don't say that, Pegeen. It gives a surge and flow to the whole room.

PATRICK. You mean there's more? (*Pegeen is off R. Auntie Mame addresses Patrick eagerly.*)

AUNTIE MAME. It's divine. Wait till you see it! Damndest thing I ever bought! (*She parts her skirt, revealing chic slacks underneath.*)

PATRICK. (*Wincing at her profanity.*) Uh—Auntie Mame, I don't suppose it's really necessary to say this—but with Gloria's folks, I hope you won't let your language get too—well, too *vivid.*

AUNTIE MAME. I won't use one teensy-weensy son-of-a-bitch all evening.

PATRICK. Good. And one other little thing. Politically, I guess you gathered they're on the conservative side.

AUNTIE MAME. I'm only wearing Republican clothes.

PEGEEN'S VOICE. (*Calling from off R.*)Could somebody give me a hand with the ladder?

AUNTIE MAME. Patrick, be a little gentleman and help Pegeen, will you?

PATRICK. (*Agreeably, as he exits R.*) Yeah. Sure. (*Agnes Gooch emerges from the kitchen, munching a canape.*)

AUNTIE MAME. Mustn't nibble on the hors d'ouvres, Agnes. You'll get fat.

GOOCH. I'm sorry, Mrs. Burnside. I try to do exactly what you say. You're so wonderful. Nobody else would have taken me in in my hour of need. I'll never be able to thank you.

AUNTIE MAME. Oh, twaddle—I'm the grateful one. You've given me a new interest—someone to look after, now that I'm losing Patrick.

GOOCH. I wish I had somebody to look after.

AUNTIE MAME. You will, dear, you will. (*Gooch is dragging*

herself up the stairs as Patrick backs through the door R., *helping Pegeen with the stepladder. He doesn't see the pregnant secretary, who stops half-way up the stairs to watch. Pegeen is carrying a tasteful but bizarre mobile.*)

PATRICK. (*To Pegeen.*) Where do you want me to set this up?

PEGEEN. Right where you are is fine. (*Patrick unfolds the ladder, and Pegeen starts up it to hang the mobile in place. Patrick looks at it warily.*)

PATRICK. What's that supposed to be, anyway?

AUNTIE MAME. (*Quickly.*) You don't like it.

PATRICK. Well, it might be a little avant-garde for the Upsons.

AUNTIE MAME. (*Decisively.*) Pegeen, take it right down. I want everything to be absolutely perfect for Patrick. (*Pegeen hesitates at the top of the ladder.*)

GOOCH. (*From halfway up the stairs.*) *I* think it's very unusual. (*Patrick wheels around as if he'd been stabbed.*)

PATRICK. What the hell is Agnes doing here???

AUNTIE MAME. (*Innocently.*) Where else would she be in her friendless condition?

PATRICK. This is one thing the Upsons simply will not understand.

AUNTIE MAME. We don't have to talk about it. Maybe they won't notice.

PATRICK. Won't notice! (*Agnes whimpers on the staircase. In the outer hallway Mr. and Mrs. Upson and Gloria appear and ring the buzzer.*) (*Panicked.*) My God—they're here!

PEGEEN. (*From the ladder.*) Help me get this thing down!

PATRICK. (*Hastily.*) No, no—leave it up! Just get the ladder out of here!

AUNTIE MAME. Norah—Ito—somebody, answer the door.

GOOCH. (*Helpfully, starting down the stairs.*) I'll get it. (*Patrick leaps toward the staircase to block her.*)

PATRICK. Oh, no you don't!

AUNTIE MAME. Now, now, Agnes, Patrick is right. (*Firmly.*) I want you to go upstairs and stay there.

GOOCH. What'll I *do*, Mrs. Burnside?

AUNTIE MAME. *Sleep*, Agnes! Knit! Read Dr. Gesell. (*The door buzzes again, a litle more impatiently. With painful slowness,*

105

Gooch starts up the stairs again. As Pegeen folds the ladder and disappears R. *with it, Ito scampers out of the kitchen and opens the door for the Upsons. Auntie Mame extends her hands in greeting.*) Welcome, welcome to the Burnside fireside!

MR. UPSON. Good to see you, Mamie! You don't look a day older. (*He laughs.*)

AUNTIE MAME. Doris—and little Glory! How I've been looking forward to this evening.

GLORIA. (*The well-bred robot.*) I cahn't tell you how pleased I am to see you again. (*This time, Auntie Mame turns the tables and gives Gloria the stiff-arm. Mrs. Upson looks around, a little baffled by the decor.*)

MRS. UPSON. My!

PATRICK. Hi, everybody. Glory.

AUNTIE MAME. Do sit down. (*The Upsons settle down in the furniture, with some difficulty. Mrs. Upson, who is no Channel swimmer, finds herself with her knees high in the air and her buttocks in the nap of the rug.*) Are you perfectly comfortable down there, Doris?

MRS. UPSON. Oh, it's so *interesting!*

AUNTIE MAME. Now, I know you're all just perishing for something to drink, after that long drive down the parkway. (*Calling.*) Ito, bring in the punch!

PATRICK. Punch? (*Mr. Babcock has appeared in the outer hallway, and rings the buzzer. Ito comes out of the kitchen, carrying a tray with a dozen or so curious, torch-shaped glasses. At the sound of the buzzer, he passes the tray with the punch bowl and glasses to Norah, who has entered behind him. Ito scampers to the door and admits Babcock. Norah passes glasses to each guest. In counterpoint to Mr. Babcock's entrance, Gloria looks up at the mobile, quizzically.*)

GLORIA. What's that *thing?*—hanging there?

PATRICK. (*Without affectation.*) It's an abstraction. Non-representational.

GLORIA. (*Girly-girly to Auntie Mame.*) Mrs. Burnside, how'm I ever going to stop this nephew of yours from using such big words?

MR. UPSON. (*As he spies Mr. Babcock in the door.*) Dwight!

MR. BABCOCK. Claude! (*Mr. Upson tries to get up to shake hands, but is having some difficulty getting out of the low furniture.*)

AUNTIE MAME. How good of you to come, Mr. Babock. (*Norah has put the silver tray down on the bar, and Auntie Mame is ladling out drinks into the torch-like glasses. Norah and Ito exit to kitchen. Mr. Babcock, moving to shake hands with Mr. Upson crashes into the mobile.*)

MR. BABCOCK. Ooops.

AUNTIE MAME. Oh dear, we'll have to raise that. (*Calling.*) Pegeen, would you bring back the ladder? (*She stops Mr. Upson from drinking.*) Won't you sit down, Mr. Babcock? Now, they're almost ready—the specialite de la maison. (*Pegeen re-enters* R. *with the ladder.*) I'm afraid you'll have to get that a little higher, dear; it's getting in people's hair. (*Pegeen sets up the ladder and climbs up to adjust the mobile.*) Oh, I want you all to meet Miss Pegeen Ryan.

MRS. UPSON. Are you the aircraft Ryans?

PEGEEN. Afraid not—just the brick-laying Ryans.

AUNTIE MAME. Claude, I'm not going to tell you one thing that's in these drinks—because all the ingredients are secret. (*She takes a long Japanese kindling-match from the table.*) Now hold still! (*She sets fire to the drink in Mr. Upson's hand.*)

MR. UPSON. (*A little stunned.*) Well, what do you know! (*Auntie Mame moves from guest to guest, igniting the drinks.*) The trick is to drink them up fast, before all the alcohol burns away. (*Auntie Mame lights another drink for Pegeen on the ladder.*)

PEGEEN. I feel like Miss Liberty. (*Patrick seems a little surprised that Auntie Mame has included Pegeen in the party, but he doesn't say anything. Each of the guests holds his drink at arm's length. They make abortive attempts to bring the glasses close to their faces, but the heat makes them thrust the torches away again.*)

AUNTIE MAME. A dear friend of mine who may drop in later calls this "The Flaming Mame."

PATRICK. (*Tensing up again.*) Who? Who? Who's dropping in later?

AUNTIE MAME. Just family, Patrick. (*Patrick looks a little like the Captain of the Titanic just after he talked to the boiler room. Mrs. Upson makes an attempt to sip her drink, but withdraws suddenly—and bats at her eyebrows as if trying to extinguish a small conflagration.*)

AUNTIE MAME. Why, don't be an old 'fraidy-cat, Doris! There's nothing to be scared of; we're fully covered by fire insurance. (*She slaps Mr. Upson on the shoulder, knowing he will appreciate the wisdom of this.*) Now, are we all lit?

PATRICK. (*Restlessly.*) Mr. Upson, wouldn't you be happier if I fixed you a daiquiri?

MR. UPSON. No, no, son. Not for a minute. Your Auntie fixed this for me, and I'm going to drink it. Why, it looks just *fine.* (*Norah and Ito come out from the kitchen bearing an elaborate tray of hors d'oeuvres.*)

GLORIA. (*Nibbling on one of the hors d'oeuvres.*) Oh, this is spicy! Try one of the little striped ones, Mums. (*Delightedly Ito and Norah pass "the little striped ones" to all the guests. Deftly Auntie Mame declines.*)

MR. BABCOCK. Say, these *are* tasty.

MRS. UPSON. (*To Auntie Mame.*) What are they, dear?

AUNTIE MAME. Just plain old pickled rattlesnake. (*The process of mastication ceases instanlty. Gloria goes into a paroxym of coughing. Helpfully Auntie Mame tries to force one of the flaming drinks into Gloria's hand.*) Why, it's pure protein. And before they marinate them, they *always* remove the fangs. (*Glancing at Babcock's drink.*) Mr. Babcock, you've gone out! (*The perfect hostess, she moves to relight his drink.*)

MR. BABCOCK. (*Waving her aside.*) Don't bother, Mrs. Burnside. (*Auntie Mame looks hurt.*)

MRS. UPSON. Mamie dear, with the wedding only three weeks away, I've just got to decide. Would you say six bridesmaids?

GLORIA. Muriel Puce had eight.

AUNTIE MAME. Then I'd say let's keep up with the Puces. (*The unseen bedroom door opens and Agnes Gooch waddles down the stairs. Patrick turns the color of skim milk. Auntie Mame addresses Gooch as if she were a puppy who had just been indiscreet on a new carpet.*) Agnes, I told you to *stay in your room!*

GOOCH. (*Whining helplessly.*) But, Mrs. Burnside, it's a quarter past eight. And you told me . . .

AUNTIE MAME. (*Quickly.*) I told you to *take your pills* at a quarter past eight.

GOOCH. But my calcium pills are in the kitchen.

PATRICK. Auntie Mame! (*Gooch painfully makes her way down the stairs and all eyes are on her. It would be easier to conceal an elephant in Bergdorf's window. No effort is made to introduce or explain Agnes, which makes the pause all the more painful and telling.*)

MR. UPSON. (*Leaning over to Mr. Babcock, confidentially.*) Is that a member of the family?

MR. BABCOCK. Damned if I know.

MR. UPSON. It's a member of *somebody's* family.

AUNTIE MAME. (*Making the best of it.*) Doris, I'd like you to meet my secretary. She's a little bit—she's not quite her*self* at the moment.

MRS. UPSON. (*Warmly, to the Gooch.*) Now, we know all about these *women's* things, don't we! (*Sympathetically.*) What's your name, dear?

GOOCH. (*Simpers.*) Gooch.

MRS. UPSON. (*Taking her arm.*) You sit right over here beside me, Mrs. Gooch. (*Auntie Mame and Patrick exchange a glance. When Gooch sits in this modern furniture she really spreads. The furniture is so low, that she sprawls completely flat.*) A little expectant mother always makes me feel weepy. I remember when I was carrying Gloria.

GLORIA. Oh, Mummy. (*Agnes reaches over and takes a canape from tray.*)

AUNTIE MAME. (*Warning.*) Now, now, Agnes—

MRS. UPSON. Remember, Mamie—she's eating for two. (*Turns back to Gooch.*) And what does *Mr.* Gooch do?

GOOCH. Oh, my father passed on.

MRS. UPSON. Oh, no, I mean your husband. (*Gooch let out a protracted wail. Both Patrick and Auntie Mame have descended on her and are helping her out of the sofa from either side.*)

AUNTIE MAME. (*Singing it out.*) Calcium time! Pegeen! (*With*

Pegeen's help, the Gooch is steered off into the kitchen. Patrick turns back to face the guests, sweating.)

PATRICK. You know, there's one thing about my Auntie Mame. She's big-hearted; whenever anybody's in trouble, she—(*The doorbell buzzes. Patrick jumps. Ito goes to the door, opens it, and ushers in Vera Charles, dripping foxes, as usual.)*

AUNTIE MAME. (*Effusively.*) Vera!

VERA. Mame, darling. Like an opening night—without critics! Heaven! (*Mrs. Upson nudges Mr. Upson.)*

MRS. UPSON. (*Lowering her voice somewhat, excitedly.*) Claude! Claude! That's Vera Charles, the famous actress, just as sure as I'm sitting here.

AUNTIE MAME. Mr. and Mrs. Upson, Miss Upson. Mr. Babcock —I want you to meet my dearest friend, Vera Charles.

MRS. UPSON. (*Under her breath*). I told you, Claude, I told you! (*Vera quickly senses that this is a matinee house.)*

VERA. (*Turning it on.*) How do you do. I'm so charmed to meet you, all of you.

GLORIA. (*Rushing up.*) Miss Charles, I've just got to tell you how I *adored* you in "Reflected Glory."

VERA. (*With a frozen smile.*) Did you, dear? That was Tallulah Bankhead.

AUNTIE MAME. Vera, can I persuade you to have a drink?

VERA. Oh, yes. Anything but rum! I've just been at the most God-awful party, and all they had were daiquiris—made with honey yet!! (*She makes a grimace and pours herself a tumbler of straight Scotch. The doorbell chimes and Ito ushers in the slightly grayed but still muscular figure of Ralph Devine.)*

AUNTIE MAME. Ralph Devine! You're a *dream* to come. (*Patrick turns away with a cramp in his solar plexis.)*

PATRICK. Oh, God.

AUNTIE MAME. Doris, you were considerate enough to show me the pictures of your little Gloria's school teachers—Miss Tuthill and all that mob—and I thought you'd like to meet Patrick's very *first* school teacher here in New York.

RALPH. (*Blandly.*) Why, Mame, don't you have a picture of me?

AUNTIE MAME. (*Easily.*) Not one we could show in mixed com-

110

pany. (*There are some eyebrows cocked at this, but Ralph floats effortlessly among the guests for introductions.* He wears a skin-tight jersey sport shirt which is open at the neck not quite to the navel. He looks at Mr. Babcock curiously.)
RALPH. Say, haven't we met somewhere before?
MR. BABCOCK. (*Studying him narrowly.*) I don't recognize the face.
PATRICK. Auntie Mame, I thought it was going to be just family tonight.
AUNTIE MAME. But you don't want the Upsons to think we don't have any friends. After all, these are the people who helped raise you. (*Glancing up at Pegeen, who seems to be having trouble with the mobile.*) Are you having trouble, Pegeen? (*Turning.*) Patrick, who don't you give her a hand? (*Patrick starts up the ladder to help Pegeen. When he gets to the top, he is in fairly close juxtaposition to Pegeen, and Gloria is not very much pleased.*)
PEGEEN. (*Nearly losing her balance.*) Ohhhhhhh! (*Patrick throws his arms around her, to keep her from falling. She grins at him.*) Thanks, Lochinvar.
PATRICK. (*Smiling back.*) Courtesy of the house.
PEGEEN. I'm okay. You've got troubles enough of your own.
PATRICK. Don't I, though?
GLORIA. (*Indignant.*) Well, that's a pretty picture, I *must* say! (*Vera decides it's time for her to go on, and she takes center stage, as usual.*)
VERA. Yes. Isn't it? Ladies and gentlemen, I want to propose a toast. (*She lifts her glass toward Pegeen and Patrick at the top of the ladder.*) To this lovely young couple, as they start up the ladder of life together.
PATRICK. (*Coming down the ladder hastily.*) No, no, Auntie Vera—*this* isn't Gloria, *that's* Gloria. (*Vera turns and finds herself staring straight into the frozen visage of Gloria Upson.*)
VERA. Pity. (*Vera downs her Scotch. The door buzzer rings. Ito moves to the door. Pegeen has succeeded in hanging the mobile, but is too fascinated by this three-ring circus to descend from her grandstand seat atop the ladder. Lindsay comes in, carrying a thick manila envelope.*)

111

AUNTIE MAME. (*Crossing to greet him.*) Lindsay, Lindsay—that's what we've needed—calm, reasonable you.

LINDSAY. (*Smiling proudly.*) I hope I'm not crashing in on anything, Mame, but I couldn't wait. I had to bring it right over.

AUNTIE MAME. What is it? (*Pleased, Lindsay hands her the envelope.*)

LINDSAY. Be careful—the ink's still wet. (*Auntie Mame draws out of the envelope the galley proofs of her book.*)

AUNTIE MAME. My book!

LINDSAY. Mame, you'll have to correct these galleys; it's your last chance to change your life.

AUNTIE MAME. (*Jubilantly waving the galleys.*) Look, everybody! I'm in print—just like Fannie Hurst! (*Vera crosses to Auntie Mame and takes some of the galleys from her, looking at them interestedly.*)

PATRICK. Congratulations, Auntie Mame. (*Patrick crosses to Auntie Mame and she puts her arm around him warmly.*)

AUNTIE MAME. Darling, I hope you don't mind, there is a lot in here about you. (*She hands him a fistful of the galleys.*)

MR. UPSON. Well, this seems to be quite a day for you, Mamie.

MRS. UPSON. An authoress! Well!

GLORIA. Patrick, you old meanie!—Why didn't you tell us your auntie was *somebody*.

RALPH. (*Crossing to Auntie Mame.*) Am I mentioned in your book, Mame?

AUNTIE MAME. Mentioned! You're *exposed*! (*She hands him some of the galleys to peruse. In fact, everybody is busy going through the galleys, except the Upsons and Mr. Babcock, who seem definitely on the outside and nonparticipants in this activity.*)

VERA. You know, I've been to so many wonderful parties here, Mame, now I'm going to find out how they all ended.

PATRICK. (*Laughing warmly as he reads one of the galleys.*) Hey, I'd almost forgotten about the time we got locked in the Mummy Room at the Metropolitan. (*He flips to another galley.*) And the time you got Miss Earhart to give me a flying lesson. (*He laughs.*) Boy, I had no talent for that! (*He flips to another galley. Warmly.*) And here's all about the roller skates. And

Uncle Beau. And that Christmas when we were so broke . . .
(*They laugh reminiscently. Suddenly Gloria claims the center of attention.*)
GLORIA. Mrs. Burnside, you could practically write a whole book about what happened to me. (*But through the babble of conversation, Auntie Mame didn't quite hear what Gloria said.*)
AUNTIE MAME. I beg your pardon, Gloria?
GLORIA. I said, you could practically write a whole book about what happened to me. (*Everybody quiets down to listen to Gloria's narrative, which she dramatizes athletically.*) Bunny Bixler and I were in the semi-finals—the very semi-finals, mind you—of the ping-pong tournament at the club, and this *ghastly* thing happened. We were both playing 'way over our heads, and the score was 29-28, and we had this terrific volley, and I ran back to get this really terrific shot . . . (*She runs back, demonstrating with an imaginary ping-pong paddle—then stops like Lady MacBeth.*) . . . and I *stepped* on the ping-pong ball! Just squashed it to nothing! And then Bunny and I went to the closet of the game room to get another ping-pong ball, and the closet was *locked!* Imagine! So we had to call the whole thing off. It was ghastly, just ghastly! (*There is another dazed pause. Vera screws a fresh drink into Auntie Mame's numbed hand, and turns her attention back to the galleys. Mame takes a long drink. Patrick comes over and takes a drink from the same glass.*)
MR. UPSON. (*With a forced chuckle.*) But it *is* amusing!
MR. BABCOCK. Yes. It is amusing
VERA. It's hilarious!
AUNTIE MAME. (*Startled.*) *What* is?
VERA. (*Deep in the galleys.*) Your story.
LINDSAY. And the most important thing, Vera, is that she did it all by herself. There isn't an Alana or a Coccamaura in the whole book. (*Agnes enters from the kitchen—Vera, whose joints have now been loosened by an alcoholic oiling, crosses to the Upsons.*)
VERA. (*Confidentially.*) You know, you'll never believe this, Mr. Upjohn, but Lindsay got this Irish slob—Brian . . . what was his name? Oh, it doesn't matter . . . to come here and live with Mame till she got the book finished. Of course, he didn't do a

damn thing except—(*She breaks off, fortunately.*) Mame, my hat's off to you! (*Agnes Gooch has been lured to the galleys, and her voice cracks as she makes an emotional announcement from the staircase.*)

GOOCH. (*Ecstatically.*) I'm so proud! The whole last chapter is about *me*! (*She reads.*) "Fighting the Stigma of the Unwed Mother!" (*She flattens out on the stairs to read. Now the Upsons and Babcock are shocked to the marrow.*)

MR. BABCOCK. (*Trying to soothe the irate Upsons.*) Claude, as soon as we get him away from the aunt, everything's going to be fine.

VERA. (*Reading galleys.*) Why, Patrick, I never realized how many times you unzipped me and put me to bed! (*There is much good-natured laughter at this but Mr. Upson takes on a righteous tone.*)

MR. UPSON. (*Standing, piously.*) Now, just a moment. We have some *young* people here.

PATRICK. (*Trying to gloss it over.*) Well, sir, I only did it when Miss Charles passed out! (*This, of course, makes it worse; the Upsons are certain that Auntie Mame's apartment is a den of iniquity.*)

GLORIA. Patrick, how can you defend people who—who—

PATRICK. (*Acidly.*) Who've never played ping-pong???

GLORIA. (*Haughtily to Patrick.*) I certainly hope when we're married you won't invite people like *this* to our house!

PATRICK. *Who* is coming to our house?—Muriel Puce and Bunny Bixler?

GLORIA. (*Regally.*) What's wrong with Muriel Puce?

PATRICK. Nothing, not a damned thing! Except she's got the I.Q. of a dead flashlight battery!

GLORIA. *WELL!*

VERA. (*Dramatically.*) Lindsay, it's marvelous. Mame's going to make a fortune from this book!

LINDSAY. She sure as hell will. But not for herself. Mame's assigned all of her royalties to the Epstein Home in Mountebank.

RALPH DEVINE. (*Interested.*) Epstein, the cellist?

MR. UPSON. What? What's that about Mountebank?

VERA. Can't the Epsteins afford their own home?

AUNTIE MAME. No, Vera, they're not going to *live* there. They're building a home for Refugee Jewish Children. (*There is a warm and favorable reaction from Mame's group.*)
MR. UPSON. (*Frigidly.*) Are you ready, Doris?
MRS. UPSON. I've been ready for quite a long time.
MR. UPSON. Come, Glory. We have a long way to go. (*He starts herding them toward the foyer door.*)
BABCOCK. Claude, please! Claude! (*Shaken, Babcock strides back into the room. He explodes vehemently directly at Auntie Mame.*) For nine years, Mame Dennis Burnside, I've done everything I could to protect this boy from your cockeyed, idiotic nincompoopery! But this is the limit. Now you've ruined everything —all my plans for this boy's future— (*Patrick is turned away and Auntie Mame reaches with her eyes to see how he has taken all of this.*)
AUNTIE MAME. (*To Babcock.*) *Your* plans, *your* plans! You have the bill-of-fare, and you're shouting orders for everybody. (*Lowers her voice.*) But did it ever occur to you that this boy might be hungry for something that you never even heard of? (*Softening.*) When Patrick walked into my life—a frightened little boy hanging onto Norah's hand—it was love at first sight. For nine years I've tried to open some windows in his life. (*She turns on Babcock.*) Now all you want to do is shut him up in some (*She reaches for the appropriate word.*) —some safe deposit box. Well, I won't let you do that to my little one! (*She stops abruptly, distantly.*) No, he's not little any more. And he's not mine. But he's not yours either, Mr. Babcock. I doubt very much that Patrick will allow you to settle him down in some dry-veined, restricted community. Make him an Aryan from Darien!— and marry him off to a girl with *braces on her brains!* (*Auntie Mame stands there, breathless, triumphant. Babcock exits. Lindsay crosses to Mame, narrowing his eyes slightly.*)
LINDSAY. Mame, did you deliberately *plan* all this?
AUNTIE MAME. (*Looking at him innocently.*) Don't be ridiculous, Lindsay. You know Patrick always makes all his own decisions. (*Patrick looks at his aunt with a crooked smile; Auntie Mame, ever the hostess, takes the center of the room with a tray of canapes.*) Rattlesnake, anyone?

PATRICK. (*To Mame.*) Thank you, Lady Iris.
AUNTIE MAME. Charmed, Lord Dudley.

THE LIGHTS FADE

ACT II

SCENE 11

Immediately following Auntie Mame's party, we hear the choral voices singing a bizarre variant on Rimsky-Korsakoff's "Song of India."

AUNTIE MAME'S VOICE. Oh, Sahib, Sahib, will you help me with this cablegram, please? Oh, where am I?
INDIAN VOICE. Punjab, India.
AUNTIE MAME'S VOICE. June 28, 19—. What year is it?
INDIAN VOICE. 1946. (*Exactly as at the beginning of the play, there is a projection on the scrim. Auntie Mame's voice is heard over the loudspeaker as the words unfold.*)
AUNTIE MAME (*Voice off.*) Mr. and Mrs. Patrick Dennis, 224 East 50th Street, New York. Dear Patrick and Pegeen. Arriving from India June 31st. Please meet me Beekman Place apartment. Uncle Lindsay off on Safari with Maharani. Means nothing. Coming back to pick up nylons, Nescafe, Kleenex, and dentures for Maharani. Only staying two days. Will explain why when I see you, because cable rates are ninety rupees per word and obviously only a damned fool would be silly enough to waste all the money on a long cablegram that went on and on and on and on. (*Her voice fades as the projection fades. We bleed through the scrim to see Patrick and Pegeen pacing in the Beekman Place apartment. The scrim flies. A tiger skin, some elephant tusks and some packing boxes are scattered about.*)
PAT. (*Calling toward off right.*) Auntie Mame, what are you doing in there?
AUNTIE MAME. (*Entering like an Indian Princess in a flowing*

116

green-blue sari.) Just giving Michael his presents, dear. (*Michael comes on holding a turban.*)

MICHAEL. Look, Dad! (*To Auntie Mame.*) Which is the front, Auntie Mame?

AUNTIE MAME. Let me do it for you, my little love. (*She puts the turban on him.*) There. Now Salaam to your mother, Michael —like Auntie Mame just taught you. (*Michael bows.*) Ahhh, very good, Sahib.

PEGEEN. That's not a real sword, is it?

MICHAEL. It's a scimitar.

AUNTIE MAME. (*Looking at her watch.*) Oh, dear! "Bell darwazay pair carr-ay ahn."

PATRICK. That's what I always say.

AUNTIE MAME. In Hindustani, that means "The water oxen are waiting at the gate." Of course, *my* ox is waiting at Idlewild. Pan American Flight 100 for Karachi. (*Crosses back to Michael.*) Oh, Michael, if I could only show you India! The splendor, the mystery, the elephants in the streets.

PATRICK. Now, Auntie Mame.

AUNTIE MAME. I know. I shouldn't even bring up the possibility of Michael's going to India with me.

MICHAEL. But Auntie Mame said she'd love to have me, she said so right in there.

PEGEEN. It's ridiculous. I wouldn't hear of it.

MICHAEL. (*He turns to his father.*) Dad?

PATRICK. Now look, it's out of the question completely. You heard your mother. (*Michael wheels on his mother.*)

MICHAEL. (*Earnestly.*) You know what your trouble is, Mom? You don't live, live LIVE! Life is a banquet, and most poor sons-of-bitches are starving to death! (*Pegeen grabs Michael and clamps her hand over his mouth, and holds him protectively. Auntie Mame and Patrick exchange a significant glance. Patrick crosses toward Michael and Pegeen. Pegeen knows that in this family you live it up to the hilt—and there's no sense in trying to resist. Helplessly, Pegeen nods and lets Michael go. Patrick steers him into the erratic but inspiring custody of Auntie Mame.*)

PEGEEN. (*A little helplessly.*) One thing you've got to under-

stand. School begins the day after Labor Day. He's got to be back
by then.

AUNTIE MAME. (*Vaguely.*) Naturally. Of course. Labor Day.
That's sometime in November, isn't it?

PATRICK. (*Firmly.*) The first week in September, Auntie Mame.

MICHAEL. (*Taking Mame's hand.*) Don't you worry, Dad. I'll
be back by Labor Day.

AUNTIE MAME. Labor! Oh, the problem of labor in India is
gargantuan.

MICHAEL. What's "gargantuan," Auntie Mame?

AUNTIE MAME. On the plane, Michael, I'll give you a pad and
pencil, and you can write down all the words you don't understand. (*Auntie Mame draws Michael toward the stairs and they
start climbing.*) Come, darling, I've been out all morning shopping for your travelling gear. Let's try things on. (*Pegeen throws
up her hands.*) Oh, I'm going to open doors for you. Doors you
never dreamed even existed. (*Michael looks up at Auntie Mame
adoringly, as they continue to climb, slowly, slowly, their eyes to
the mountain tops.*)

PEGEEN. My God, she's the Pied Piper!

AUNTIE MAME. Oh, what times we're going to have, my little
love. What vistas we're going to explore together. First we're
going to see the Taj Mahal, which is one of the Seven Wonders
of the world— (*They go off together toward that adventure of
life, and we know what a banquet it is going to be for both of
them.*)

THE CURTAIN FALLS

For curtain calls, Norah and Ito come out with trays of
champagne glasses. Then the entire cast stream in through the
foyer door, each taking a champagne glass and toasting the
audience. Young Pat-Michael reaches for champagne, but Pegeen
gently slaps his hand and gives him a glass of milk instead, with
which he toasts the audience. Once they are all on, they turn
their glasses and toast toward the steps, down which Auntie Mame
comes, and bows like an Indian Princess.

118

AUNTIE MAME'S COSTUMES

The clothes Mame Dennis wears should make every female theatre-goer yearn for such a wardrobe. But the couturier must realize that Mame is no mere clothes-horse. She wears daring gowns exactly as she wears preposterous people and astonishing events. Her taste should be a superb combination of elegance and insanity. In the original Broadway production, Miss Russell's gowns were designed by the late Travis Banton, who achieved brilliant effects, and each new entrance brought a gasp from the audience. (If the budget for your production is modest, put it on the star's back!)

Some of the changes are very quick, and require underdressing as indicated. In other instances, changes are made while she is playing a scene. Mame needs well-oiled zippers, and the well-rehearsed co-operation of a skilled dresser who can work in the dark.

Here is a resume of Mame's wardrobe, scene-by-scene:

ACT I

Scene 3: Mame's entrance is in an outlandish Chinese robe of black silk embroidered with gold and scarlet smacking of the late Twenties. Her wig is black, closely bobbed. She wears pajamas which will be retained in the following scene, which requires a fast change. In this, her Scott Fitzgerald period, she should be accessoried to the hilt—with rings, jeweled slippers and assorted Chinoiserie.

Scene 4: Mame discards the previous embellishments, including the wig, and has about 40 seconds to kick off the slippers and put on a pair of fluffy mules; a flimsy negligee replaces the previous embroidered robe. She comes down the stairs still wearing a sleeping mask, which she cocks onto her forehead like Mr. Lindbergh's goggles. A rack of bizarre gowns is brought on as a prop during the action. Mame chooses one into which she changes off-stage during the action. It is a tailored suit, which she wears with trim street shoes and the most restrained jewelry—in sharp contrast with the eccentric ostentation of Scene 3. She now wears a wig or fall which has been braided into a "halo."

Scene 5: This is a fairly quick change. The "halo" is discarded, and Mame enters dripping with silver fox and wearing a smart cloche hat of the period. She can be wearing the same suit, but the hat, furs and accessories should disguise the fact.

Scene 6: Mame is underdressed with a plain "basic black" dress, which she will wear as a working girl. But this is totally covered with a striking scarlet job (which appears in all the show posters); this is a full skirt, ankle length, Mame in her most dramatic magnificence. The costume jewelry jangles noisily.

Scene 7: Mame is zipped out of the scarlet gown and emerges in a lightning swift change as a telephone operator. (She can begin the lines as the telephone operator in the darkness while she is stepping out of the previous dress. Here she is in plain and simple black, no accessories.)

Scene 8: Add a white collar to the "basic black" for the Macy's scene. Have a plain cloth coat ready for her cross into:

Scene 9: She remains in the same dress.

Scene 10: Mame transforms herself into a Southern belle—donning a Scarlett O'Hara-ish wig and a bouffante dress billowing with petticoats.

Scene 11: She makes the change into riding habit while playing the scene with Pat, who sits on a bench outside the Dutch window. Here the attire is white shirtwaist with ruffled front, a twill riding skirt and trim jacket, a black stove-pipe riding hat and boots that have been carefully prepared so that they will flop at the ankles, making it seem that Mame was never able to get her feet fully into them. She carries a riding crop.

Scene 12: Mame changes into a torn and dirty version of the riding costume for her final scene of the Act.

ACT II

Scene 1: Young Pat only.

Scene 2: Mame is seated on one of the steps of the Pyramids, dressed in a beige duster suited for tropical travel, possibly with pith helmet.

Scene 3: Older Pat only.

Scene 4: Mame throws a huge fur parka over her tropical gear, so that the change is almost instantaneous. The parka has a fur hood, which frames her face.

120

Scene 5: Mame has ample time for this change into haute couture widow's weeds. The dress is a slinky, form-fitting black, over which she wears a fur-trimmed black coat; she carries a matching fur muff. She has wigged herself with a streak of gray—which, at first, is concealed by a very discreet black hat and a black net veil. Concealed beneath the coat is the fact that the back of the seemingly austere dress is bare, slashed to the waist, with a deep pink rose, artificial, at the point of cleavage just above her derriere.

Scene 6: Again, she has ample time to make the change into her Charlotte Bronte mode. The dress is full-skirted dark green vetlvet with tailored collar and cuffs. The wig is severe, more closely trimmed and without a trace of gray; the accessories are nil—for now she is the working authoress.

Scene 7: Same dress.

Scene 8: Mame does not appear.

Scene 9: Here is Mame in her most elegant restraint, impressing the Upsons with a superb tan chiffon. Mame's sophistication and taste must be in sharp contrast to the gaucherie of the Upsons. She has discarded the previous wig.

Scene 10: There's not much time for this change, but she must be stunning in a gold lame skirt slit up the front to reveal sleek black jersey pants and a jersey top. She wears a collar of rhinestones and a vivid red belt. In short, she is dressed to the hilt—and slightly beyond it.

Scene 11: Mame's hair, over the interval, has gone to a carefully selected blue-gray. She is dressed in high-caste Indian fashion, complete with a blue-green sari and all the baubles of a maharani.

*   *   *

PROPERTY LIST (does not include furniture)

Pads of paper
Pencils
2 suitcases
Vases
Artificial flowers, pots, ivy, etc.
Magazines (1928)
2 cigarette boxes
Ashtrays—3 living room; 2 foetus-shaped
Will
Xmas presents—a. rhinestone bracelet in box; b. perfume bottle, cologne and bath salts in box; c. wristwatch in box; d. long pants in box
Long bamboo cigarette holder
Telephones old-style
　1 French (cradle) telephone with 20-foot cord
　5 Manhattan glasses
　8 Martini glasses
　9 Old-fashioned glasses
　8 jiggers
　14 highball glasses
Silver ice bucket
Cocktail tray
Cocktail towel
Liquor bottles: Gin, Vermouth, "Southern Comfort," Bacardi (1 pint and 1 quart), Scotch and Brandy
1 wooden ladder
1 light metal ladder
Roll wallpaper
Wallpaper brush
Model airplane (on card & stick)
2 nut bowls

Waste bowl for bar
Cocktail pitcher (glass)
Cocktail stirrer
Cocktail napkins
Sleeping Mask
Hairpin box
Hairpins
Assorted hair switches (different colors)
1 Switch; partly braided
Breakfast tray
Cup & saucer
2 Prop Dresses: A. Green velvet (wardrobe); B. Bright green with fringe (wardrobe)
Negligee on hanger (wardrobe)
Biological chart on easel
Groceries in shopping bag
Tortoise shell glasses
3 packages wrapped in wrapping paper
Large box tied with string
2 feather dusters
Make-up tray
Small hand mirror (on theatre make-up tray)
Towel
Powder puff
Telephone switchboard: Earphones, Mouthpiece, Dial, etc.
Handbag (wardrobe)
Compact (in this handbag)
Roller skates & roller skate boxes
Waste basket
Sheaf of bills on spindle spike
Corsage
Xmas tree

Xmas tree decorations including one detachable
Holly over mantle
Poinsettia
Macy's sales book with pencil
Tinker Toy
Package (Xmas-wrapped)
Stage money
Soda tablets in bottle
Parasol (wardrobe)
Book—"HOW TO RIDE A HORSE"
Riding crop (wardrobe)
Camera with flash attachment (practical!)
Silver tray with 7 silver punch cups
Hunting Horn
Field glasses
Cane (Ma Burnside)
Hand bandage (made up to slip over hand)
Lace handkerchief
Steering wheel
Gun in holster
Red Fox
Desk blotter
Letter (longhand)
Alpinstock (rigged with rope)
2 camera cases
Camera case with camera & trick film
Extra cushions (for height on chair behind desk)
Dictaphone with earphones
Shorthand pad
Text books
Typewritten letter

Typewriter
Large pile of manuscript sheets
Manila folder (pencil & steno pad in folder)
Thin volume of poetry
Small package wrapped in white tissue
Lederhosen wrapped in white tissue with steamship labels (wardrobe)
Alligator jewel case
Fur wrap
Door key
Silver cocktail shaker
3 silver daiquiri glasses
Tray of prop canapes with edible canapes in center
Jar honey
Bottle lemon juice
Towel
Breakfast tray
Dummy egg in cup
Mobile on wire
Tray of striped (edible) canapes
Silver tray (large—double pecker-wood)
Manila envelope with galley proofs
6 Trick parfait goblets (Sterno/Salt mixture)
Tiger head
Scimitar
Ice cubes
Muslin for dust sheets
Fireplace matches
Photograph album
Punch bowl
Turban

"AUNTIE MAME"
ACT I - SCENE 5

CHU CHIN CHOW

WORDS & MUSIC BY
LAWRENCE & LEE

I'm a chu choo girl from chu chin chow, and how and how I'd

love to chin and chew with you; and turn the skies to blue with you- and twen-ty three ski-

doo with you! Chu chu chee chee chow chow and how! and how! and how!

"AUNTIE MAME"

ACT II - SCENE 1

ST. BONIFACE FIGHT SONG

WORDS & MUSIC BY
LAWRENCE & LEE

Fight! Fight! Fight! for St. Bo - ni - face - Bo - ni - face!

We will win for St. Bo - ni - face! Bo - ni - face.

Car - ry the ball o - ver the line. Show 'em what we can do.

Fight! Fight! Fight! for St. Bo - ni - face blue.

"AUNTIE MAME"
ACT II - SCENE 3

O RUMSON U

WORDS & MUSIC BY
LAWRENCE & LEE

O Rumson U, dear Rumson U., to thee we'll e'er be staunch and true. E'en

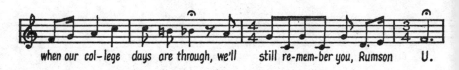

when our col-lege days are through, we'll still re-mem-ber you, Rumson U.

ACT II - SCENE 6

TU-RA LOORA LAY

WORDS & MUSIC BY
LAWRENCE & LEE

Tu-ra loo-ra lay, a loo-ra lay, a too-ra loo-ra lay; tu-ra

loo-ra lay, a loo-ra lay, a too-ra loo-ra lay.

NEW
PLAYS

THE LIGHTS
by Howard Korder

THE TRIUMPH OF LOVE
by James Magruder

LATER LIFE
by A.R. Gurney

THE LOMAN FAMILY PICNIC
by Donald Margulies

A PERFECT GANESH
by Terrence McNally

SPAIN
by Romulus Linney

Write for information as to
availability
DRAMATISTS PLAY SERVICE, Inc.
440 Park Avenue South   New York, N.Y. 10016

NEW

PLAYS